Melinda — Thank you for your Wisdom! ~md

Advance Praise for ...

How to Lead Without Alienating, Bullying, or Destroying Your Team Book Materials

"**Great and Needed Workshop!** How to Lead Without Alienating, Bullying, or Destroying Your Team gave our team the opportunity to learn techniques to better our organization and spearhead our leadership growth with applicable takeaways and actionable concepts to better identify opportunities to influence an attitude of excellence from all team members. So much value and insight - should be a required workshop for all leaders and organizations!"

~Ms. Brenda Lawrence, Director Program Quality
District 27 Toastmasters International,
Fall Conference 2017

"**How to Lead Without Alienating, Bullying, or Destroying Your Team** is a great book! Full of straightforward and practical advice, this powerful, easy-to-read book, challenges readers to examine their leadership behaviors that can destroy and divide organizations. A recognized leadership and management expert, Dr. Gillam's latest work provides insights for leaders who value the respect and trust of their team members. Her strategies for building an organization that reflects an inclusive leadership style is priceless, and a crucial read for leaders in the 21st century."

~Ron Monk, Senior Global HR Professional
Certified Global SHRM-SCP

D1403327

"The <u>key</u> to how to lead without alienating, bullying, or destroying your team is to guard your tongue with what you say, and evaluate your actions by what you do."

How to Lead Without Alienating, Bullying, or Destroying Your Team

Strategies for Organizational Success

"The hallmark of authentic leadership is a leader's ability to build and transform not alienate and divide."

How to Lead Without Alienating, Bullying, or Destroying Your Team

Strategies for Organizational Success

Dr. Mary M. Gillam, Col (Ret), USAF

Amazon #1 Bestselling Author

Ordering Information: All books are available on Amazon, most bookstores, and via the author's business website at https://www.executiveleadershipbiz.com

Printed in the United States of America
Book Cover: Background Image, "Group of Diverse Hands Together" (#52314496) purchased from 123RF, LLC Stock Photos. Concept and idea to overlay author's photo on top of the diverse hands was done by a freelance designer at Fiverr.com.
Author Photo: Jackie Hicks, Fond Memories Photography

For additional books by the Author and booking information:
Website: https://www.executiveleadershipbiz.com
Business Email: info@executiveleadershipbiz.com
Additional Email: Dr.MaryM.Gillam@gmail.com

Dedication

To all of the men and women who desire to lead without alienating, bullying, or destroying your team.

To all of my encouragers, supporters, mentors, and coaches who inspire me to excellence.

Thank you for being part of my life-long journey to build leaders and change lives!

"Leaders are the architects of the organization. They provide the building blocks for either team cohesion or team destruction."

Contents

List of Figures

Preface

How to Lead Without Alienating, Bullying, or Destroying Your Team is a book that I hope every leader will read. Why? Because, too many organizations are being destroyed due to toxic leadership behaviors.

As leaders, this paradigm must change. Since you hold the *key* to the change that must occur, then it must begin with you. As the architect of your organization, you provide the building blocks and the cultural foundation for either team cohesion or team destruction.

With organizations facing a crisis due to allegations of misconduct across the board, then the time for training in behavioral modification is now. The spotlight is on, and it is at maximum wattage. There is no grace period.

Leaders must become emotionally responsible for their roles, actions, conversations, and their decisions leading to this turmoil. If you are going to lead from the front, then you need to learn how to avoid the pitfalls of aggressive and venom-laced leadership.

The hallmark of authentic leadership is a leader's ability to build and transform not alienate and divide. For the success of your organization, you have to recognize the difference between the two. Your ability to succeed at the former is paramount.

Although some may argue that tough or aggressive

leadership is not workplace bullying, but holding people accountable and responsible, I would argue that a leader's communication style, motives, and intent can make a world of difference. Your ability to communicate without destroying a person's self-esteem in the process, is a sign of a leader who values emotional intelligence, team unification, and positive organizational culture.

As someone with first-hand experience with leaders who practiced aggressive leadership behaviors that morphed into workplace bullying, I want to see this behavior stop. There is no room in the workplace for bullies. However, some leaders need help in recognizing and changing those behaviors that alienate, bully, and destroy teams.

Filled with practical advice, actionable strategies, sound research, and numerous real-world stories, this easy-to-read book will help you, the leader to avoid leadership tactics that destroy careers, and embrace those behaviors that transform teams and change lives.

Acknowledgments

Thank you to Ms. Brenda Lawrence, and District 27 Toastmasters International Fall Conference participants for allowing me to share my research and data on this topic with you. Your positive feedback and enthusiastic comments inspired me to take the research to the next level and complete this project.

I owe a debt of gratitude to all of my sisters and brothers who were willing to listen, and beta test many of my theories and ideas. You inspire me more than you will ever know.

I also want to thank every professor, boss, colleague, employee, and friend who has enabled me to write this book. Along life's journey, you learn things that can either make you give up or move up. Because of your inspiration, I chose to move up.

Finally, I would like to thank my God, the giver of all wisdom, for allowing me to write a book designed to help leaders transform from a mindset of negative self-indulgence to a mindset of positive team-governance.

"Don't allow your ego to take you pass your ability to see the value in others. The same individuals that you snub today, may be your bosses tomorrow."

Introduction

The Gig is Up!

Over the past several years, leaders at every level have come under scrutiny. Unruly behaviors, attitudes, and activities, which were once ignored have now taken center stage. No longer are the rants, tirades, and out-of-control outbursts of leaders permitted to continue to pass as camouflaged leadership.

Without argument, great leaders lead. Yet, when a leader's behavior results in the alienation, bullying, and destruction of the team, then "Houston, we have a problem, and it is not with the space shuttle."

It is time for a behavioral modification intervention. This intervention cannot be deterred or delayed. Why? Not only does the leader's negative behavior affects the health and well-being of the team, but the organizations' bottom-line. Profits and losses can be directly affected by the behaviors of organizational leadership.

Several months ago, a prominent Chief Executive Officer (CEO) of a major company resigned due to a series of outbursts that went viral. His behavior was deemed inappropriate. The impact on the company was immediate demanding that the CEO step down. The CEO would later assert that he needed leadership development training.

After reading much of the commentary on the case, it was alleged that the company had a very toxic work environment. According to the press, several lawsuits had been filed by employees based on workplace bullying and harassment.

This company is not alone. Leaders can either make or break an organization. Numerous studies suggest that many organizations are now in crisis mode trying to rebuild and reclaim their reputation, organizational culture, workforce, client-base, and industry standing.

Yet, in order to move the organization forward, requires leaders with the capacity to acknowledge their problems and transform their behaviors. There is an old adage that says, "A person cannot fix, what he or she is unwilling to acknowledge."

> "A leader is not defined by his or her willingness to act when everything is good, but by his or her willingness to act when everything is at stake."

False self-perceptions often leave leaders at a disadvantage. They prevent you from seeing personal behaviors that may require modification or change. Leaders determined to grow, must be willing to change.

2

How to Lead Without Alienating, Bullying, or Destroying Your Team is a book designed to help leaders recognize and avoid the toxic behaviors that can ruin and derail organizations. If you are a leader who wants to grow and take your leadership to the next level, then this book is for you. It will challenge you to rethink how you lead.

Although the book is not a recipe for instant change, it is a great leadership development training resource because it comes from a place of knowledge. Not only do I understand leadership and management theory, but I have coupled book knowledge and research with real-world leadership and management hands-on experience.

Having spent over 30+ years in telecommunications, information systems technology, and cyber security leadership and management senior positions, I know what it takes to build *award winning* teams whose mission impacts the entire organization. I have dealt with aggressive personalities and had to implement change under pressure cooker conditions. I understand leading from the front, because it is more than just a trendy slogan.

As a former government Senior Executive Service (SES) member, and former Chief Information Officer (CIO), I was constantly in the hot seat. Not only was I responsible for the insertion of new technologies (visionary), development of enterprise-wide software and hardware architectures, establishing cyber-security policies and procedures, but also the daily operations and maintenance of current technology infrastructures.

I guess you can say that I was a member of the

science, technology, engineering, and math (STEM) movement before the term was ever announced. In addition to leading military units, I have led organizations comprised of government employees and contractors. Likewise, I have served as the chapter president for numerous not-for-profit organizations, and have served on several Executive Boards. In addition, I am a certified John Maxwell Team Speaker, Coach, and Trainer.

By drawing on a wealth of knowledge collected from many sources, this book will inevitably provide leaders with actionable information that can help them to lead without destroying their team.

The book is divided into two parts. In Part I, I discuss *The Horrible Sting of Workplace Bullying*. After providing some basic definitions of key terms, I address the question, "Where Does Bullying Start?" Using primarily real-world stories to present some terrible truths, I then invite readers into the lives of victims who suffered alienation, workplace bullying, manipulation, sexual harassment, and other atrocities at the hand of their boss or the individual exercising power over them.

In Part II of the book, I discuss *Strategies for Organizational Success*. These strategies are designed to help leaders transform their leadership behaviors, and avoid creating toxic work environments. Throughout the chapters, I include real-world stories addressing behaviors that leaders should avoid in order to take their organization to the next level of peak performance.

To further enhance the learning experience, I also include what I call *Lightbulb Moments*, which are key lessons learned from the various chapters.

Part I

The Horrible Sting of Workplace Bullying

"How do you measure work-life-balance when a key component (work) is out of balance? No one should have to endure horrid and stressful working conditions that result in alienation, bullying, manipulation, or coercion."

1 -Time for Change

And Why It Matters Now?

I have a secret. I must confess. When I agreed to speak at the District 27 Toastmasters Conference in Arlington, Virginia, little did I know that this event with hundreds of attendees would lay the foundation for my next leadership book. As I began to prepare, I thought, "What aspect of leadership can I share with this distinguished group of professionals and colleagues?"

Then I experienced a *lightbulb* moment. Having earned a Masters in Executive Leadership at Georgetown University (GU) in Washington, DC., I had the privilege to research and study a host of leadership, management, and organizational development topics that were impacting organizations and keeping executives awake at night. So, which one of these topics would prove to be the elephant in the room? If you guessed *workplace bullying,* you are correct.

Numerous studies suggest that workplace bullying

remains a serious problem. Despite all the training, regulations, policies, protocols, and processes, workplace bullying continues to threaten the internal fabric of organizations around the globe. From toxic and stressful work environments to low productivity and high employee turnover rates, the negative effects of this behavior are destroying organizations. It is time for *"supersonic" change.* Organizations can no longer turn a blind eye to this problem and leave it to various departments to resolve. Change must start at the top.

> According to the Workplace Bullying Institute, 19% of Americans are bullied while another 19% witness the behavior.

So, what can be done to combat this problem? Are leaders contributing to this toxic behavior? The answer is a resounding "yes."

Why I Wrote the Book

As a former victim of workplace bullying at the hand of a supervisor, and a colleague, I am intimately familiar with the adverse effects of this behavior. In addition to the stress and humiliation, you often feel isolated and alone, especially if the bully is your boss. On many occasions, I was on the brink of tears, but I stood my ground. Although, I eventually left the position for another job, the interpersonal blemishes or scars from the bullying remained for years to come.

By leveraging my personal experience and research, I wrote this book so that I can help leaders (at every level) learn how to lead without alienating, bullying, or destroying their team. Since many of my Georgetown University cohort members were in leadership positions, I had the opportunity to gain diverse perspectives on workplace bullying. It does not matter what position you hold, you can fall victim to this behavior.

Testimonies from District 27 Toastmasters

With my topic now solidified, I knew that the District 27 Toastmasters Conference would be a great place to present my research on *How to Lead Without Alienating, Bullying, or Destroying Your Team.*

As the host and executive producer of the local television show, *Leadership Table Talk,* I knew that I needed to begin my conference presentation with a major hook. What would it be?

I thought, "How can I connect with the audience? How can I capture their attention, maintain their focus, and land the plane?"

Since I knew my idea was worth sharing, I could not afford to blow my opening. I decided to go for gold with several enrolling questions.

"How many of you have ever completed a resume? Can I see a show of hands?" As you can imagine, every hand in the audience went up.

"Now let me ask, how many of you have ever put on the resume, I alienate, bully, and destroy teams?" Not a single hand was raised. Complete silence.

Although the latter question was a jaw dropper and rather extreme, this type of leadership behavior is pervasive in organizations. Leaders using intimidation, manipulation, and harassing tactics have been documented throughout history. The recent #hashtag movements are just a few examples of victims taking a stand declaring—no more.

Since the conference presentation laid the basic foundation for my book, I introduced the audience to several new concepts:

- Leadership FOG©
- The 3D Leadership Syndrome©
- The Know Factor of Leadership©
- Are You a Dr. Jekyll or Mr. Hyde Leader?
- 4-Step Communications Model©
- The 3L Listening Model©

The response to the material was over-whelming. Based on the enormous positive feedback, I knew that I was addressing some major leadership and team-building issues. For example, *bully-clad* leadership is not leadership.

Nodding in continuous agreement, many attendees acknowledged that some of the behaviors described several leaders in their respective organizations. This acknowledgement confirmed much of my earlier research. Poor leadership behaviors remain an incessant threat to organizational cohesiveness.

My objective at the conference was to leave the audience with innovative, thought-provoking, and actionable information that they could use and apply immediately.

At the conclusion of the presentation, several attendees asked, "Do you have a book documenting the information that you presented today? If so, where can we purchase the book?"

To an author and researcher, these questions were music to my ears. Yet, I had a problem. Since I had not finished the book, my unfortunate response to the audience was, "Not at the moment, but it is in progress." Although I was an Amazon #1 best-selling author of several books, I had not completed this particular book.

However, to continue validating my research, I presented some of the materials at a different keynote presentation at the Belle Haven Country Club in Alexandria, Virginia. Following this presentation, one business owner wrote,

> "Dr. Gillam not only provided several useful tools on effective leadership communication to our business group, she did so at a TED Talks level of quality with clarity, authenticity, and a personal story, all of which created a compelling and memorable message for the attendees."

Given the overwhelming feedback to this material, I knew that I had to make this information available to a broader audience. Whether you are a novice or seasoned leader, I invite you to read this book. I encourage you to take time to conduct a self-analysis of your personal leadership style.

For example, how would you respond to the following questions?

1. Is your leadership style sabotaging your organization's growth?
2. Do you lead from a place of integrity?
3. Are your leadership skills, competencies, and behaviors adding or subtracting from the team?
4. Does your team follow you because they respect you or is manipulation and coercion, the <u>root</u> of their trust?
5. How are your communications and listening skills?
6. Do you cringe at the prospect of someone offering an opinion different from your own?
7. What is the size of your ego?
8. Is your character worth emulating? Would your team agree with your assessment?

Although these questions are self-reflecting, I trust that as a leader, they will challenge you to think about the example that you are presenting to your team.

2 -Where Does Bullying Start?

D id you know that 61% of workplace bullies are bosses? This alarming statistic was published by the Workplace Bullying Institute in 2017. See Appendix A for more findings. This statistic serves as a somber reminder of how rogue leaders and managers can use their power and influence to destroy individuals and organizations. Since bullies typically seek to exercise a form of control (e.g. intimidation, manipulation) over their target, they must be in a position to inflict pain.

Bullying Defined

What is bullying? Although there are different categories of bullying (e.g. workplace bullying, classroom bullying, cyberbullying), there are some basic elements that apply across the board. According to the preponderance of the literature, bullying is aggressive or focused negative behavior toward a single target or multiple targets, repeated over time, with a goal of

Alienation

Isolation or separation from a group or an activity to which one should belong or in which one should be involved.

Bullying

Aggressive or focused negative behavior toward a single target or multiple targets, repeated over time, with a goal of inflicting physical or emotional harm.

Destruction

The act of destroying or damaging something to the extent that it no longer resembles its original form.

Figure 1: Key Definitions

inflicting physical or emotional harm on the victim.

Constant criticism of an employee's work performance for no apparent reason can be a sign of bullying especially when it is done in an open forum.

Some individuals stated that their bosses possessed a certain degree of bias toward them. They would praise co-workers for equivalent level work, while criticizing or minimizing their contribution. These individuals felt as if they were singled out for harassment and humiliation.

Early Warning Signs

Where do bullies come from? Do people wake up one morning and decide they want to become a bully? The answer to this hypothetical question is no. Although I am not a psychologist, I understand that certain behaviors are learned over time. For example, when babies are born, they have no concept of hatred or bigotry.

Yet, as *negative influencers* began to shape their world view, these innocent babies grow into adulthood with learned behaviors rooted in misguided perceptions. Unfortunately, they began to act on these behaviors which at times can manifest in their supervisory roles. Imagine having one of these individuals serving as your boss—your teacher, your team lead, or even the company president.

Although this book is not a treatise on bullying, I want to address some of its characteristics. For example, some bullies wear disguises, making it difficult to identify them—initially. Their persona may shock you. In some cases, the individual instigating the bullying is the last person on earth that you would have ever expected.

The following story will introduce you to whom I

15

will describe as the "subtle" bully.

The Subtle Bully – Kia's Story

The little girl (whom I will refer to as Kia—which is not her real name) was only ten years old when she experienced her first taste of classroom bullying. Being taller than the other children in her class, Kia was extremely self-conscious.

"If only I was shorter," she would often say. "Maybe then I would fit in, and not feel isolated—alone." Then the unimaginable happened.

The bell rang. The teacher motioned for the students to take their seats. As she began calling the roll, the students waited in anticipation for their name to be called. Upon hearing their name, each student would respond with either "here" or "present."

Yet, when the teacher approached Kia's name, the teacher made a horrific joke. For some unknown reason, the teacher chose not to call Kia by her proper last name, but used an *animal descriptor* to identify the young girl.

The teacher added "key" to the child's last name. Instead of calling Kia Dunn, the teacher said, Kia Dunnkey, which to the class sounded like **Kia Donkey**.

Hearing this horrible blunder, the majority of the students erupted into uncontrollable laughter. Even the teacher, who was charged with setting the right example for the students, engaged in the ridicule.

Now, think back to when you were 10 years old. Put yourself in Kia's place. Imagine how she must have felt hearing the giggles. She was at the heart of their laughs.

Broken and confused, this child should have never had to experience the pain that strikes at the very core of a person's identity. No matter how strong you may appear to be, words can and will hurt at any age. The classroom was not a stage, and the situation was not a play.

As she looked around …

Tears began to swell up in Kia's little brown eyes. Feeling the devasting weight of this embarrassment, she wanted to get up and run out of the classroom, but she could not. There was no escape. She was stuck — nowhere to go.

How could the teacher be so callous and insensitive? What could have convinced her that this joke was acceptable? Her careless behavior had a huge impact on this child's life.

For Kia, her classroom experience would never be the same again, and her life would change forever. She had become the laughing stock of her class. On numerous occasions, students would call Kia by the name that was inaptly given to her by *"the teacher."*

So, what message did the teacher convey to these elementary students who would one day become adults? Bullying, disrespect, harassment – are all acceptable behaviors. It never crossed the teacher's mind, that she had deeply offended the little girl.

When an adult (e.g. teacher) instigates and condones ill-advised behavior toward others (e.g. students), it is reasonable to assume that some of the audience members (e.g. fellow students) will mimic the adult's behavior. This is exactly what occurred in this classroom experience.

When interviewed by psychologists, many bullies have confessed that their bullish behavior did not just materialize in adulthood. It was learned overtime. As a child, they pushed the envelope. Their behavior eventually became more aggressive and repetitive. Their goal was to inflict a degree of harm either physically, emotionally, or mentally on their target(s).

Motivated by pride, power, or greed, bullies feel a sense of entitlement. They are the headline in their own narrative. They gravitate toward power, and will challenge anyone who tries to disrupt their perfect union of self-embellishment and pride.

Now, let's look at the messages that Kia received from the teacher, who in this story was the *subtle bully*.

> "I am worthless. Nobody cares about me."
>
> "My feelings don't matter."
>
> "Since the teacher did it, I have no one I can go to for help."

For the remainder of the school year, Kia had to endure the taunts. The snickering that occurred behind her back was heart-wrenching. According to Kia, she was emotionally and psychologically affected by the name-calling for years. Being tall, quiet, shy, and reserved, she had already felt isolated and alone. This incident increased her pain and eroded her self-esteem. Yet, Kia chose not to allow this situation to define or chart her course in life. She chose to <u>forgive</u>.

Lightbulb Moments

In summary, what lessons can leaders learn from Kia's response to the bullying that impacted her life? Some would argue that Kia could have taken her pain and turned it outwardly and became a bully *herself*.

There are many studies that suggest that some people who were bullied, gravitate toward this behavior for revenge. By inflicting pain on others, they attempt to cloak, cover, or hide their lingering emotional scars.

However, Kia selected a different path. Let's look at what she did, and how leaders can learn from her response.

- **Service-before-Self**. Despite her pain, Kia chose to turn the heartache of bullying into a life-long experience of *helping and serving* others. In her local community, she became known for extending a hand to those in need. Although she did not have much, she did not allow that to stop her from putting others first.
- **Self-esteem, respect, and dignity matters**. By

finding inspiration and motivation from a host of sources, Kia chose to reclaim her self-worth and self-esteem. Kia knew that she was greater than any word spoken about her. Sometimes, you have to rise above the negative influencers and reclaim who you were meant to be.

- **Derail the bully**. When victims of bullying succumb to the bully, they empower him or her to continue their pursuit of reckless behavior. However, when victims strive to rise above this toxic behavior, they regain the position of power. They are no longer the victim, but the victor.

According to famed psychologist, Abraham Maslow, as humans we have certain needs that motivate us to performance. Self-esteem is one of those needs.

While the other four needs (physiological; safety and security; love; and self-actualization) are equally important, it was the self-esteem need that motivated Kia to push pass the criticism and pain of her youth to become a woman of excellence, honor, and character.

> **"When we are willing to forgive others and choose not to live in the hurt and pain of yesterday, we become the bigger person!"**

Although, Kia is no longer with us in this life, I honor her memory by sharing her story. I am proud that she did not surrender to the bully. She instead chose to turn her negative bullying experience into a positive life transformational message. We can all learn from Kia's story and how she chose kindness over revenge.

Learning Forgiveness from President Nelson Mandela

As I was finalizing this chapter, I began to think about my trip to South Africa in 2016. Although I had been to the African continent as a Political-Military Adviser on several occasions, this trip was different. While in South Africa, I got the chance to visit Robben Island where the late South African President Nelson Mandela spent 27 years in prison.

When it comes to a miscarriage of justice, Mr. Mandela had every right to be bitter. As a political prisoner, his basic right of free speech was revoked. What we may take for granted in the United States with our First Amendment Right, Mr. Mandela was unfortunately prohibited from engaging in public discourse. Based on his treatment, he could have easily developed a hatred for those who had placed him in prison. Yet, he chose forgiveness instead.

When I think of Mr. Mandela, I am reminded of the four universal ethical principles: autonomy, beneficence, non-maleficence, and justice that were part of my studies in Dr. Mike McDermott's class at Georgetown. As a man who fought against apartheid, Mr. Mandela believed in autonomy or self-rule. He fought for justice and the fair treatment of all. He was a man of courageous principles.

Despite his imprisonment in body, he never surrendered to becoming imprisoned in the "mind." As a man of strong faith, Mr. Mandela chose to forgive his enemies and to advocate for a Rainbow Nation that recognized everyone.

Mr. Mandela encouraged South Africans to act in ways that did not inflict harm to others. He also proposed that South Africans show kindness, acts of mercy, and charity. Some may have thought that Mr. Mandela was a dreamer to think that people would forgive those that had oppressed them for years.

Yet, President Mandela, like Dr. Martin Luther King, Jr., had a dream of a better tomorrow — and a brighter future for his country.

While in South Africa, I also got the privilege to visit the Mandela Rhodes Foundation (MRF), which provides scholarships to deserving South Africans. Having the opportunity to meet Shaun Johnson, the MRF Executive Director was an amazing experience because he personally knew Mandela and was able to elaborate on many of the stories written in the *Long Walk to Freedom: The Autobiography of Nelson Mandela*. Because of his willingness to advocate for Mandela's freedom, Mandela entrusted Johnson with his first interview after his release from prison.

Given the background of Cecil Rhodes, it was interesting to see the combination of the two high profile leaders partnering together to create a dynamic leadership capacity in Africa. With the Mandela Rhodes Foundation, Mandela chose to lend his name to a foundation that would seek to reconcile the past, and offer hope to the future.

3 -Leaders Gone Awry

Monday began as a great day. I was excited to start working with my new client. As a I approached the office complex, my tranquility was dashed by a loud voice thundering through the hallway.

The Mad Director

"Get in here now," screamed the irate and agitated man. "I need those figures. What kind of staff are you? Are you too dense to understand deadlines?" Sprinkling a few expletives throughout the one-way conversation, he continued his rampage on his staff.

Toxicity filled the air. You could have cut the tension with a knife. Papers being shuffled and people hustling, everyone was scrambling to get to the meeting. Despite the emotional turbulence, it was apparent that no one wanted to be late.

Shocked and confused, I whispered to the receptionist, "Who is that, and does he act like that all the time?"

To my dismay and horror, the receptionist replied, "He is one of the directors, and yes, that is his normal behavior." This man was more like the *"Mad Director."*

Can you imagine how the staff must have felt going into that meeting? Place yourself in their shoes. Forget about being pushed under the bus, this staff has just been crushed by the unrelenting verbal assaults of an out-of-control boss. I could not help but wonder, "Is the staff really like this, or did the director simply forget to eat his Wheaties?

Although I was just passing through this work area to get to my workspace, my conscience was seared by this leader's emotional disposition, and this unhealthy conversation. With over 30 years in leadership and management, I know the difference between leaders who build teams, and those who destroy them. This director did not earn my vote for director of the year. This leader had obviously gone awry, and his bullish tactics did not endure him to his team. He could have used a course on *Leadership and Emotional Intelligence.*

> "Everything rises and falls on leadership!"
>
> - Dr. John Maxwell, Renowned International Leadership Expert

You may wonder why did this episode bother me?

Let me explain. Having served on the Air Force Inspector General's team in the Pentagon for several years, I investigated numerous allegations and cases of leader misconduct. Given my investigative background, I was shocked that this director was permitted to treat his team in such a bullish manner.

Since **NO** leader is above the law, how was this director permitted to continue in his position? Did he intimidate the staff? Were they afraid to report his abusive conduct? Something was not right here.

If the director's inexcusable behavior was common knowledge, then somebody dropped the ball. The director had a boss. He had peers. Yet, no one was willing to act.

Impact on the Team

Based on ongoing conversations with the staff member, I detected that the morale was extremely low in the organization. The directorate had an enormously high turn-over rate. People were constantly leaving. The work climate created by the director did not foster cooperation but isolation and alienation.

Apparently, this director confused his position with authentic leadership. In his book, *The 5 Levels of Leadership*, New York Times #1 bestselling author, Dr. John Maxwell reminds us that "true leadership isn't about position." Although this director was in charge of the organization, he lacked the leadership persona required to build a positive work environment. However, since the director had been in the position for a long time, changing his behavior and mindset toward his team would be an uphill climb.

If one tenant of leadership is influence, then who is this director influencing with his bullish behavior? What kind of example is the director setting for future leaders? This director had a responsibility to conduct himself in a manner conducive with proven leadership principles. Hollering and screaming at employees is never the correct solution to any problem. This behavior only further alienates the team and cripples the organization.

Imagine, if all the pieces of this work puzzle had been aligned properly, then this real-world case study would have never made it into this book.

Bully Undercover – Gary's Story

Let's look at another case in which the leader went awry. In this scenario, the leader was obviously afraid that his subordinate's performance would overshadow his contributions to the organization. As a consequence, the leader began to publicly demean the individual forcing him to leave the company.

For years, Gary (not his real name) believed that he was the heir apparent to his boss. He had worked hard and knew the operations inside and out. His efforts had generated much revenue for the company. Because of his commitment to excellence, his outstanding work had gained the attention of upper management. In many organizations, this is viewed as a great accomplishment. For Gary, unfortunately, this is where the awkward problem began.

Gary's boss was not ready for retirement. However, now that Gary has begun receiving numerous accolades from senior management, his boss became resentful. Based on his follow-on actions, it was apparent that he had begun to play out a series of *what-if* scenarios in his head.

"What if Gary gets promoted over me?"
"What if I am forced to retire because the company wants to promote him?"
"What if my boss wants Gary to now start accompanying me to meetings with him?"
"What if Gary's work is deemed more valuable to the company than my contribution?"

Although one can only speculate if Gary's boss was actually pondering the above questions, it was obvious that something had changed. When Gary spoke to me about his situation, he was unclear as to what drove the change in his supervisor's demeanor toward him. Despite receiving praise from senior management, Gary was certain that his boss was not happy with his new-found fame. He resented it.

Without any warning, Gary's supervisor began reducing his workload.

Workplace bullying is gender neutral.
Numerous studies suggest that men and
women are vulnerable to unscrupulous
leaders who choose to bully rather than lead,
mentor, or coach

No longer was Gary receiving the high-profile projects. Despite having expertise in some of the biggest projects in the company, he was no longer being asked to participate in key decisions. Work that at one time was deemed the best in his area, was now being marginalized.

On several occasions, Gary's boss criticized his work publicly. He began to humiliate him and question his competence. Gary felt as if he was working for a boss of many faces. Because his demeanor changed so drastically, Gary felt compelled to speak with him.

Despite speaking with his boss, Gary noticed that nothing changed. The stress of the work environment was now starting to affect his work-life-balance. He could not sleep and his wife was beginning to wonder about his health.

The actions of Gary's boss were creating enormous pressures for him for no apparent reason. The unjustified harsh treatment and criticism was unwarranted. Having received outstanding evaluations previously, Gary was convinced that his boss was trying to sabotage his performance and his standing in the company. Having no other recourse, Gary decided to approach the human resources department. Although he was pleased with their willingness to help him, he knew that this would be a long-term major pursuit for justice.

The Invisible Man

After filing his complaint, Gary returned to his office. Although he had hoped that things would have never reached this point, he had no choice. Unfortunately, he would continue working for the same boss while the investigation was ongoing.

"Invisible" does not begin to describe how Gary was treated upon his return to the office. The person who was once deemed heir apparent was now treated like a pariah. Yet, he had done nothing wrong. Imagine being punished and rejected for simply doing a great job.

However, if Gary thought he had been *marginalized* prior to the complaint, his boss now began to ignore him completely. Not only did the boss disregard him, but several of his co-workers (who were good friends with the boss) followed suit. The same co-workers who Gary had worked with over the course of several years have now joined forces with the boss to humiliate him. There are studies that suggest that some employees will bond with the bully to prevent becoming the bully's new target. It is difficult to determine if the coworkers were actually against Gary or afraid of the boss.

Effects on the Company

In his heart, Gary believed that his boss wanted him to *quit the company*. Overtime, the boss felt threatened by the skills and talents that Gary brought to the table. After having Gary's skills noticed by upper management, Gary's boss began to question his own position in the company. These are signs of a leader's insecurity and immaturity.

Unfortunately, Gary's boss did not know how to cope with employees who were more than just one-job wonders, but had the potential for greatness. Gary was a rising star, exceptional employee, who was deemed a threat versus an asset by his boss.

Instead of celebrating the fact that upper management was recognizing one of his subordinates, Gary's boss became jealous. This jealousy would produce seeds of distrust, anger, confusion, and disrespect. The biggest loss from this unfounded jealousy is that this company eventually lost a great employee. There is a high price to be paid when great talent walks out the door.

Although Gary was contemplating filing a lawsuit, he could no longer cope with the bullish tactics from his boss. The stress was too much for this talented giant—destined for more. After discussing the matter with his family, and securing a job elsewhere, Gary submitted his resignation and quit.

His skills would no longer be lost on a boss that failed to recognize or appreciate the talent within his organization. In the end, some may say that the bully won, but when it comes to one's health and family, leaving may be a small price to pay. No job or amount of money is worth an early grave.

Lightbulb Moments

In summary, here are some of the lessons that leaders can derive from these two case studies.

- Leaders who act as bullies and go awry create a hostile work environment.
- Leaders who elect to use language full of

toxicity and venom are <u>not</u> leaders but are merely occupying a space.

- Leaders who alienate and bully others create a dysfunctional organization.
- Leaders who abuse their position, establish a revolving door for talent departure.
- Leaders who are not secure in their own leadership ability will resent employees who threaten their position in the company.
- Leaders who are "self-centered" versus "team-centered" can negatively impact the entire company. Their decisions will focus on their needs and wants at the expense of doing what is in the best interest of the company.

Now that we have looked at workplace bullying through the eyes of individuals who experienced it first-hand, let's now explore some specific strategies that can help leaders avoid the subtle pitfalls that create toxic work environments and destroy organizations from within. These strategies are designed to help leaders recognize and forego behaviors that foster division, disruption, and discord.

Part II

Strategies for Organizational Success

4 -Strategy #1
Resist Leadership *FOG*

W hen I mention the word *fog*, what comes to mind? Cloudiness, reduced visibility, dense weather conditions are probably words, that ring off your tongue. According to the Oxford dictionary, fog is "a thick cloud of tiny water droplets suspended in the atmosphere at or near the earth's surface which obscures or restricts visibility."

You are now probably wondering, what does fog have to do with toxic leadership? What a great question. Let me explain.

When it comes to leadership, some leaders develop behavioral blind spots. They cannot see past their perception of themselves. The only voice that matters to them is their own especially if someone else has a differing opinion.

These individuals are so absorbed with themselves that they abdicate or relinquish their role as an authentic leader. As their inflated ego increases, so those the cloud of deception. Without an intervention, these leaders enter into what I describe as the FOG Zone, not the Twilight Zone, but the FOG Zone. In this case, FOG is described as:

- F = False Humility

- O = Obsessed with Power

- G = Guided by Ego

Just like natural fog, this phenomenon obscures a leader's vision, decision-making, and mindset. Given the attributes of this type of FOG (which has to do more with personal attributes than the weather), these leaders are more destructive than productive.

False Humility

Leadership FOG is a by-product of leadership deception which is grounded in pride and arrogance. Leaders who fall victim to leadership FOG engage in hubris behavior and the psychological trap of "over confidence." There is nothing wrong with having a positive self-image, or confidence in your abilities, but when those things cross the line of self-aggrandizing, then, it is time for a major reality check.

When leaders have an embellished self-portrait of themselves, they can easily alienate and bully employees through their self-centered, exaggerated belief that they are better than their team.

So, what is the opposite of unpretentious humility? The answer is *false humility*. When I wrote my first books on leadership, I conducted a survey and ask participants to identify characteristics or qualities that they admired in leaders. "Humble" was the word many respondents used as a genuine quality that they appreciated in their leaders. Yet, history is full of leaders who ascended to a certain level and threw humility out the window along with the bath water.

For these leaders, there is an invisible "I" in team. Unfortunately, leaders who fall victim to FOG are the only ones who can see the "I" in team. It is present in their mind only.

False humility can surface in many ways. For example, leaders who display false humility may appear to shun the spotlight, fame, or glory. Yet, their actions and their behaviors reveal a different mindset. These leaders may even advocate for the team, using a plethora of trendy verbiage, but in the final analysis, it is all about the leader.

Let's take a look at a hypothetical example. Suppose company X achieved its financial projections for 4th Quarter Fiscal Year 20XX. This success was made possible by the hard work of a particular business unit. In recognition of this achievement, a C-level executive makes a special appearance to the business unit.

As recognitions are being made, the business unit leader acknowledges his team but in a perfunctory or superficial manner. Every comment he makes is laced with his own personal contributions versus that of the team. The business unit leader speaks about the team as if they were merely an "afterthought."

In his New York Times bestseller, *What Got You Here Won't Get You There*, Marshall Goldsmith identifies 21 transactional flaws or habits that can derail leaders. As I read through the different habits, I was drawn to Habit #10, which was "failing to give proper recognition." This habit clearly describes the actions of the business unit leader. Although, the leader appears to be team oriented to a certain degree, he is only focused on his specific rising star.

Leaders who are not genuine, but practice false humility make decisions based on the what's in it for me (WIIFM) matrix. For example, this leader may respond to his or her staff with this kind of self-centered message,

"I know we are a team, but if any specific actions are going to impact my reputation or embarrass me in the organization, then we need to revisit this proposal. I am not going to put my neck on the line for anybody."

Although the good of the organization should be paramount, these leaders are self-motivated. If their actions contribute to personal gain, then they will march full speed ahead. For these leaders, their perception of reality is based on their lens alone.

Leaders who desire to lead without alienating, bullying, or destroying their team, should view humility as a virtue and not a weakness. The fact that you are entrusted to lead either your own private firm or a public organization requires a genuine servant's heart.

In his book, *Outstanding! 47 Ways to Make Your Organization Exceptional*, John Miller writes, "Humility is a key trait of outstanding organizations—and of individuals. It allows people to communicate more freely, creating a culture of authenticity and accountability." What a profound observation. Imagine, if every leader would embrace these statements. There would be no need for toxic communications or bully pulpits. These tactics only produce a divided workforce and misguided leader.

Obsessed with Power

Does power have the ability to corrupt leaders? Have you ever met a leader obsessed with power? Can the abuse of power create schisms in organizations leaving employees alienated and bullied by senior authority?

Power, according to one definition is, "the capacity or ability to direct or influence the behavior of others." Given this definition, one could surmise that power, placed in the wrong hands, used for the wrong purpose can corrupt an individual.

While researching a speech on charisma and influence, I discovered a book by Kurt W. Mortensen entitled *Maximum Influence*. The author of several outstanding books, Mortensen is a principal authority on persuasion, negotiation, an influence. Although I was drawn to the book because of the author's discussion on charisma, I found myself engaging in several of Mortensen's publications.

In 2009, Mortensen wrote the article, *Command*

Attention with Power and Authority. In this article, he discusses several tenants of power. As I read the article, I was captivated by his proposition that "…power is a neutral force. It can be used for great good — to inspire and to uplift — as well as for coercion. The good or bad quality comes from the person who is exercising it."

Now, let's look at some recent behaviors that have taken the abuse of power to the nth level. Not only have lives been impacted by this egregious behavior, but many *victims* have suffered in silence. For reasons that we may never understand, these victims were singled out for abuse, torture, humiliation, and destruction. Although it was not their fault, they became the pawn in the hands of the person wielding the power.

What's in a Hashtag?

In 2017, high profile sexual harassment scandals riveted the airways. This narrative became international. No country, government, or organization was off limits. From the halls of Congress to Hollywood, trusted leaders and people with enormous power were accused of doing the unthinkable, causing many to wonder if power corrupts. Even while finalizing this book, there were several allegations being made against key individuals that span the course of decades.

Since sexual harassment is defined by the U.S. Equal Employment Opportunity Commission (EEOC) as "unwelcome sexual advances, requests for sexual favors, and other verbal or physical harassment of a sexual nature," then leaders can use their power to manipulate and coerce employees into behaviors that demean and demoralize. Although sexual harassment has existed in the workplace for years, recent #hashtag movements have empowered many victims (both men and women) to come forward and confront their abuser.

On a personal note, although I was never sexually molested, I personally know several individuals who endured this hurtful and despicable act. For years, they suffered in silence—revealing this horrendous trauma to nobody. The toil that it took on their lives was almost unbearable. Hate and bitterness tried to keep them from fulfilling their God-given dreams and destiny. The aftermath of the assault(s) left a legacy of brokenness that the perpetrator could have never imagined. Yet, these individuals were determined not to allow the perpetrator to win. With God's help, they were able to reclaim their lives. Although it has been a day-to-day journey, they are still surviving.

A few years ago, I spoke about *Stopping the Violence* which dealt with sexual abuse victims. As I encouraged the audience to get involved in helping to recognize and eliminate this abuse, I did not realize the profound affect that it would have on them. After the presentation, I had several people to thank me for continuing to sound the alarm on such a sensitive topic. Unfortunately, several of these individuals had also been sexually abused.

Although this book was not originally going to delve into sexual harassment, I could not complete this manuscript and not address one of the most critical topics dominating our airways today. We all know that power in the hands of morally bankrupt individuals can alienate, bully, and destroy lives. For example, some leaders abuse their position by coercing, manipulating, and forcing people to do things that they would otherwise not do. Exercising calculating, shrewd, and cunning tactics, some leaders will boldly ask, "If I do this for you, what will you do for me?" This behavior is especially prominent in organizations were there are enormous generational gaps.

Leaders obsessed with power can use their authority or position to try and manipulate or persuade junior team members to engage in adverse, deviant behaviors. This scenario has not only played out in organizations worldwide, but at many military recruitment stations. Several years ago, the media was flooded with young women coming forth and sharing their stories of threats, coercion and manipulation.

Regardless of the nature of the behavior, or the level of the leader, individuals who abuse their power, authority, and position are not fit to lead. It will only be a matter of time before their behaviors destroy the organization. Power hunger leaders are not made to last, but will eventually meet their match. As Morrison aptly states, "When power is abused, it will lose the ability to persuade and influence."

So, as a leader, do you wear power as a badge of honor? Do you lead from a place of personal or positional power? Has your treatment of power impeded your relationship with your organization? In answering these questions, I hope that you will recognize the neutrality of power.

Power, in and of itself is not destructive. It is only when leaders abuse power that it becomes a force of dishonor especially when *immoral* favors become the currency of choice.

As a leader, if you want to truly earn the respect of your team, don't become obsessed with power. Recognize power for what it is. If you use it wisely, then power will *never* become the measuring stick by which you inadvertently reward and punish unfairly.

Guided by Ego

Do you have an inflated ego? On a scale from 1 to 10 with 10 being the highest, how would you rate your ego? Now, if I asked members of your organization to rate your ego, do you think the numbers would match? Your perception of you, and their perception of you can reveal much about your leadership.

Now, think, suppose your ego is creating a divide in your organization. For example, how would you like to be described as "conceited, self-centered, arrogant, or self-absorbed?" These are a few of the words used to define egotistical, whose root word is ego. These words can also be the foundation for creating a leader who is not a team player, but an independent actor pretending to lead with nobody in tow.

Leaders who want to lead without alienating, bullying or destroying their teams cannot afford to allow their ego to take center stage in how they treat employees or run the organization. Some leaders, for example, may choose to act in ways that promote their abilities while diminishing the contributions of others.

Yet, leaders who are not ego-centric but team-centric,

resist the temptation to build a personal shrine to themselves. They prefer to have others recognize their contributions and worth to the team. These leaders are not motivated by ego but by positive actions and behaviors that produce lasting impact.

Leaders destined to create sustainable value consider their opportunities to lead as platforms for helping others to grow and develop while advancing the goals of the organization.

When Ego Subverts Action – Carla's Story

Let's look at the story of Carla who was the leader of a large organization. Although Carla had worked hard to get to the level in which she served, she had adopted some bad behaviors along the way. When asked about how she arrived at her leadership position, the conversation would always end 20 minutes later. If you did not have time to listen, then don't ask her to tell the story. Carla had an ego that would rival anyone whose mission was to dominate the spotlight.

Unfortunately for Carla, her ego would one day generate some major problems at her job. On several occasions, her team had informed her about a specific issue that needed to be resolved quickly. Because Carla thought that action on this issue would highlight problems in her work area, she chose to delay action and dismissed her team's recommendation. Then the unexpected happened.

Everything hit the fan! The specific issue that Carla chose to ignore repeatedly, got the attention of her boss. How was she now going to explain her position?

Later that day, Carla's boss approached her about the matter. He was mortified by her lack of action to resolve the issue. You do not need to be a rocket scientist to know that this situation (which could have quickly been resolved) did not end well for Carla.

In Carla's quest to protect her image, she made some major leadership blunders. Her flawed judgment and inactivity ruined her reputation as being a proactive problem-solver. The actions that got her to the place of growth were being overshadowed by her pride, arrogance, and ego.

It was apparent that Carla had changed, and not for the better. It was time for a reality check—not a reality show (humor), but a serious reality check.

Leaders, if you allow your ego to circumvent your decision-making, then your value system is flawed. You need to reassess what leadership is and is not. Leadership is not based on your title or position, but it is characterized by the positive example that you consistently set for your team.

Lightbulb Moments

In summary, here are some of the lessons learned from this chapter.

- Fog, as a weather condition is acceptable, but not as leadership behaviors.
- Great leaders resist leadership FOG.
- Leadership FOG does not produce the kind of teambuilding results that sustain organizations.
- Being humble does not equate to weakness. It

43

reflects a leader's ability to remain grounded. No leader achieves his or her position alone.

- Misuse of power, position, and authority can devastate individuals and teams; create a false sense of identity; and destroy organizations.
- Don't let an inflated ego lead to your downfall. It can not only enlarge your head, but also your fall.

If I was to sum up this entire chapter with one quote, I would reference the international bestseller book, *Leadership and Self-Deception*, published by the Arbinger Institute. In the book, the authors warn leaders about the fallacy of self-deception. They write, the "...key to leadership lays not in what we do, but in who we are..."

So, if you want to lead without alienating, bullying or destroying your team, <u>resist</u> leadership FOG.

5 -Strategy #2
*A*void *The* 3D *L*eadership Syndrome

Are you a leadership hazard? Are you the kind of boss that thrives on chaos? Is your organization in crisis facing a major team disruption? What kind of work environment are you creating? Does your team enjoy working for you or are you a negative influence?

Discord, Dysfunction, Disillusionment

If you answered yes to any of the above questions, then you may unfortunately be the kind of leader who promotes *discord, dysfunction, and disillusionment* among his or her team. These three factors comprise the 3D

Leadership Syndrome. See Figure 2 below. They are not conducive or beneficial to team cohesiveness, leadership development, or organizational growth.

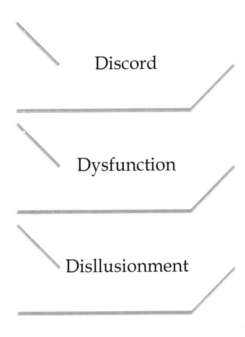

Figure 2: 3D Leadership Syndrome

These ineffective leadership elements will destroy your team. For example, employees who genuinely want to produce for the organization will not continue to tolerate what they perceive as discord and dysfunction. They will eventually become disillusioned with the organization and make their voices heard.

Let's take a look at a story that depicts these three non-productive elements.

The Heartless Bully - Karen's Story

Karen was so excited to start her new job. She was eager to show the boss what she could do to add value and help the organization achieve its goals. After being in the organization a few years, Karen began to notice that everyone was getting promoted except her.

When she spoke with her boss, she was immediately sent to speak with another individual who had no direct involvement in her supervision. She was puzzled about this direction, but she did not want to create any tension or make any waves.

However, as time went on, Karen noticed that she was being singled out for different things. She was even accused of not being a team-player. Although she had never been told this before, she felt that her interest in getting promoted has opened a door that somehow her bosses wanted to keep shut. She was totally confused by their irate behavior.

Despite the opposition, Karen continued her quest to get an answer. However, as Karen begins to explore other opportunities within the organization, she began to realize the level of discord that existed in her organization. It was dysfunctional, and the leaders were a major part of the problem. They contributed to the discord and the confusion.

On one occasion, Karen stated that some of the leaders did not have the necessary leadership development training required to lead the teams. They were placed in positions in which they were not prepared to handle the immense and diverse people related responsibilities. One could speculate that this organization would probably not make the *Best Places to Work* list.

After weighing her options, Karen decided to take her talents to another company where she was valued, respected, and appreciated. When Karen submitted her resignation and told her boss why she was leaving, it was as if he was surprised that she would want to leave their organization. Despite his lack of support for her future advancement, he acted as if she was unappreciative of her job. He appeared angry that she no longer wanted to work for him. He was taking her desire to leave as a personal assault on his leadership.

At that moment, Karen realized just how heartless her boss was. His initial refusal to answer her directly when she first asked about her promotion potential revealed a lot about his inability to communicate effectively with his team. In many ways, it was a direct reflection on his lack of leadership development training.

For Karen, if she had remained in the organization, she was never going to get past her boss' bias perception of her or her abilities. Although he knew that she was talented, he had some major inner flaws that kept him in his own internal prison. As her boss, his leadership actions (or lack thereof) directly affected her ability to get promoted within the organization.

Even though, we sometimes pretend that these negative leadership behaviors don't exist, and that all people are treated fair and equally, that is not the case. Unfortunately, there are individuals serving in key leadership roles at various levels who are unable to appreciate a diverse workforce. Their personal biases can create barriers in their decision-making and prevent them from doing what is right. Although, sometimes these individuals are subtle in their flagrant actions, at other times they are very blatant.

Since Karen's boss did not hire her directly, he was not invested in her growth or promotion potential. She was merely a team member that he inherited with his leadership position — nothing more, nothing less.

Emily Morrison, author of *Leadership Skills: Developing Volunteers for Organizational Success* warns that when leaders misuse their implicit power, employees will either fight back, remain silent, or take flight. One of these three actions is going to occur. In Karen's case, she chose to take flight.

Realizing her worth, Karen recognized that she had more to give. She was not going to allow this negative work experience to prohibit her from moving forward. Karen knew that her talents and skills were in demand. She was ready to move to an organization that would enable her to grow, develop, and soar.

Lightbulb Moments

In summary, what are some of the key take-aways that leaders can learn from this chapter?

- Leaders who create discord, dysfunction, and disillusionment within their organization will reap the rewards that follow such turmoil.
- There are numerous studies that suggest that when the work environment is toxic and employees are under-valued, and under-

appreciated, they seek opportunities elsewhere especially millennials. This group of highly skilled talent is refusing to limit their skillsets to organizations that undermine their contributions.

- Employee turnover rates are now becoming a by-product of an organization's established culture.
- A leader's bias can cloud his or her judgment.
- Leaders with limited leadership development training can create discord and dysfunction due to their lack of knowledge and experience in leading teams.

6 -Strategy #3

Conquer the Know Factor

of Leadership

Building a successful team starts with leadership. Integral to this assessment is that you must first know who you are as a leader. John Wooden, famed, legendary head coach at the University of California at Los Angeles (UCLA) once said, "The most powerful leadership tool you have is your own personal example."

There are **three** knows that every leader should know if he or she wants to lead without alienating, bullying, or destroying your team. For example, if you are a world-class athlete bound for the Olympics, then you are expected to know your body, know your sport, and know the rules and regulations governing the industry.

Although most leaders may never become Olympic hopefuls, you can excel in the leadership position that you occupy. When you invest time in learning about the three knows depicted in Figure 3, you will discover that you are on the verge of building an organization that will last. But first, the learning begins with you.

Figure 3: The Know Factor of Leadership

This point was epitomized by Joe Gibbs, former head coach of the Washington Redskins and a member of the National Football League Hall of Fame. I had the privilege of being stationed in the Washington DC metropolitan area when Gibbs coached the Redskins. The example that he set before his team and the community inspired many to pursue their dreams. A man of enormous faith (which inspired me even more),

Gibbs remains well-loved in the Washington DC metropolitan area.

In his book, *Racing to Win: Establish Your Game Plan for Success*, Gibbs writes, "Building a winning team starts with the man or woman in your mirror." If you can't lead the complex individual that you see every time you pass a mirror, then you will have difficulty leading the myriad of personalities that you will encounter on your leadership journey.

Getting to Know You

What kind of leader are you? I am not asking if you are transformational, transactional, or charismatic? What does your <u>character</u> say about you? Do your team really know who you are? Are you a Dr. Jekyll or Mr. Hyde, or are you a leader whose reputation conveys quality, excellence, integrity, honesty, respect?

In his book, *The 15 Invaluable Laws of Growth*, Dr. John Maxwell writes, "Your view of yourself determines behavior. One will never outperform their self-image. The value we put on ourselves is the value others will put upon us...The first person you need to <u>lead</u> is yourself." However, in order to lead yourself, you must first know yourself.

Are You a Dr. Jekyll or Mr. Hyde Leader?

Several years ago, I had the privilege to give the keynote address at the Tysons Regional Leadership Conference. During the presentation, I used a movie analogy to emphasize the importance of understanding a leader's character and behavior.

In the 2014 Hollywood thriller blockbuster movie, *The Equalizer*, world-renowned actor, Denzel Washington plays Robert McCall, a *mild-mannered supervisor*. He works at a local Home and Garden store. Yet, McCall has a "secret."

No one really knows the real Robert McCall. As the movie progresses, McCall begins to privately reveal different aspects of his character. Although there are external extenuating circumstances that drive these changes, the point is that McCall remains a mystery to his team.

On the surface, McCall appears to be a quiet, and wholesome man. His outward persona is that of a well-organized, no-nonsense boss. As the movie continues, the real McCall steps out of the shadows of his past and begins to act in accordance with his **real** character.

As I watched the movie, I begin to think about Robert Louis Stevenson's novel, *The Strange Case of Dr. Jekyll and Mr. Hyde*. Published in 1886, this novel describes the inner struggles of dueling personalities residing in one body. The novel's main character, Dr. Henry Jekyll is constantly battling his inner personality (referred to as Mr. Edward Hyde) to remain in control of his faculties and his behaviors.

Now, how does Stevenson's 1886 novel relate to this 2014 movie? As described earlier, Robert McCall is battling secrets. Although McCall's outward persona reflects that of Dr. Jekyll, his true character and behavior is more akin to Mr. Hyde. McCall struggles to keep his real character at bay. Yet, it is difficult to be

Dr. Jekyll, when Mr. Hyde is dying to come forth.

So, as a leader, what is your **true** character? Are you guilty of presenting two different versions of you to your team, or to the public? Are you a Dr. Jekyll or Mr. Hyde leader?

In getting to know you, let's look at several thought-provoking questions. How would you answer these questions?

1. When your team speaks about you, what adjectives or characteristics are used to describe the real you?
2. Does your behavior reflect a person of character, honesty, integrity, and respect?
3. How do you treat your staff, your peers, and your boss?
4. Have you created a work environment that fosters teamwork?
5. Have you established a reputation that makes you an ethical leader worth following?

Leaders destined to lead without alienating, bullying or destroying their team values the importance of their character, name, and reputation. In getting to know you, it is critical that you value these elements as well.

For example, when your name is mentioned in diverse forums, how are you perceived? Leaders build their reputations every day. We have all heard the adage, "Your reputation proceeds you." You are either known as a person of honor or dishonor.

I am reminded of the bible verse that says, "*A good name is rather to be chosen than great riches and loving favor rather than silver and gold"* (Proverbs 22:1, KJV). So, what does your name really say about you?

Build an External Network

Leaders destined to lead effectively, do not work in isolation. They do not allow stress to cloud their judgment. Every leader needs an outlet to vent.

Don't allow your frustrations to build up and you take them out on your team, your family, or even your dog. Build a team of like-minded leaders who can help guide you through your leadership challenges. As you get to know yourself, you will learn that you are not alone as a leader. Become organized in your search to connect with other leaders.

Sometimes, it may take having another pair of eyes examine something that you have struggled with to add a degree of clarity. Use your network so that you can gain different perspectives on critical issues. You will be surprised at who in your network just dealt with the same issue, and may have the perfect solution.

Find a Coach or a Mentor

Everyone is familiar with the importance that coaches play especially in sports. Yet, coaches are also important in helping individuals improve their leadership performance. The right coach can inspire and motivate you to change your behavior especially if it is problematic. He or she can coach you through scenarios or situations that may be prohibiting you from being your best self. Don't be afraid to ask for help.

When it comes to finding a mentor, choose someone that you admire and displays the qualities that make them qualified to mentor another. This individual should be someone who can help you get to that next level as a person of values, integrity, honor, and respect.

Getting to Know Your Team

Leaders, your ability to <u>communicate</u> and <u>listen</u> to your team will enable you to get to know them. In their 2017 Global Human Capital Trends report, Deloitte researchers note that *"...42% of companies cite leadership development training as a top priority."* If you are able to master your communications and listening skills, then you can move your leadership abilities from *good to great.*

Communications Does Matters

Whether you are discussing your vision, mission, objectives, or employee performance, communications at the right time, place, with the right people is essential. Fundamental to this assertion is this, *if you fail to communicate with your team, you plan to fail.* To get to know them, you have to communicate with them.

However, there are some communication activities that can hamper a leader's ability to connect with his or her team effectively. After making the case for communications, I need to address the elephant in the room. **How** you chose to communicate to your team is as important as the communications itself.

Several years ago, I worked as the Military Assistant to the Under Secretary of Defense, Comptroller for the Office of the Secretary of Defense (OSD) at the Pentagon. During that time, the Secretary of Defense or SECDEF, would send special notes to his senior staff called, *Snowflakes*. Because I served on the *personal staff* of the Comptroller, I worked a lot of these notes for my boss.

When your office received a *Snowflake*, there was power associated with that note. You knew the note required immediate attention. Regardless of the content of the note, or the "ask", the recipient was required to act immediately.

As leaders (especially senior leaders), there are some **key** questions that you should ask before you hit the send button. By asking these questions, one can minimize confusion, reduce the number of repeats that occur when the wrong question is answered, and get a more informed response.

Because you value and respect your time, you should also value and respect the time of your team. Respect is earned. It is a two-way street.

Four Questions to Ask Before You Draft the Note

1. Is this note necessary? Is this note worth my asking my people to stop – take action – respond!
2. Is the purpose clear? Leaders must consider the time, resources, and energy required answering their inquiries. Make the "ask" as clear as possible.

3. What is the anticipated response? Depending on the content of the note, the response can generate a *positive or negative* impact on the recipient.
4. Is the method of transmission appropriate?

The Power of a Note - Whitney's Story

Whitney was about 12 years old. She lived with her grandmother. One day, after arriving home from school, Whitney found a note posted on the door of her grandmother's house. The *note* was addressed to her grandmother who was not home. Letting her curiosity get the best of her, Whitney decided to read the note, which was from her school. It said, *"Although your granddaughter is a very good student, she tends to talk a lot, which at times is very disruptive to our classes. Unfortunately, if she does not change, we are going to have to send her to a reformatory school."* For those of you who may not know what a reformatory school is, it is a place where kids are sent who are deemed to have behavioral problems. As Whitney continued to read the note, tears began to swell in her eyes.

"How can this be? My teachers like me," proclaimed Whitney.

Yet, the note was real. For Whitney, not only had she disappointed herself, but she had now brought shame on her family. What was she going to do? Imagine how Whitney felt reading that note about herself.

As a leader, how can Whitney's story help you to better communicate with your team regardless of the issue? Let me answer that question, by asking this,

"How many of you value your self-esteem and self-worth?" I anticipate that your answer is yes to both. Since you value your self-esteem and self-worth, that would imply that others probably value their self-esteem and self-worth as well.

In returning to Whitney's story, was there another way that the school administrators could have conveyed the message to Whitney's grandmother? For example, are some conversations more appropriate for face-to-face communications? If Plan A fails (e.g. the grandmother was not home), then have a Plan B (e.g. ask the grandmother to come to the school, call, or try to reach the grandmother on another day. Don't just leave a note that can be found by anybody).

As leaders, when you are contemplating sending a *contentious* note to someone, especially one that may challenge their performance, remember that the person on the receiving end of that note is not a robot, but is a real person – with real emotions.

The Emotional Divide

In 1995, psychologist, Dr. Daniel Goleman wrote a book titled, *Emotional Intelligence*. In his book, Goleman discusses the need for individuals to recognize not only their emotions, but those of others. As you take your emotions captive, you can adjust your decision-making and activities based on present emotional information. In today's vernacular, I would suggest that it is being in the moment or presence with your emotions.

Leaders **never** send a note when you are angry. You

may regret it. Step away from the computer. An ill-advised communication can destroy an organization.

Although you may delete a negative note from the computer, you cannot delete it from a person's memory bank. People have long memories, and don't mind sharing information around the physical water fountain or via the electronic water fountain (social media). The "grapevine" remains alive and well.

Before You Hit Send: The 4-Step Communications Model

Leaders, before you release your next angry communication, I recommend that you walk through the steps of my 4-Step Communications Model in Figure 4. As you are considering your actions, review this model.

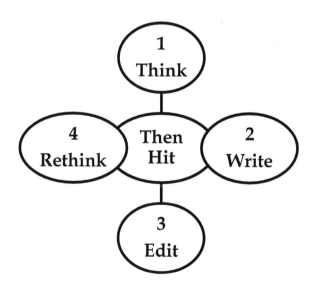

Figure 4: 4-Step Communications Model

This model asks you to do four things: think, write, edit, and rethink.

1. **Think**: Contemplate about what you want to say. Don't just send a note because you can without any regard to the person receiving the note. As the leader, your words matter regardless of how, why, when, and to whom they were sent.

2. **Write**: Visualize your comments by writing them down on paper or your computer. What do you see? Rage, anger, hostility, are these the words that you want to send? Is this the message that you want to convey?

3. **Edit:** Review the text that you have written. Is there a better way to get your point across without destroying the recipient? Once you have finalized your decision, eliminate any unnecessary verbiage that adds no value or confuses the matter. Be clear, be brief, and be direct.

4. **Rethink:** After completing steps 1 through 3, ask yourself this question, "Does this matter require a note or some other means of communications?" It never hurts to rethink a matter especially if it is contentious.

As leaders, my challenge to you is this, "When you decide to send a note, I hope that it will not demoralize, defame, or infuse a situation, but motivate or inspire the recipient of the correspondence to change for the better.

Listening is Key

In the introduction to this book, I indicated that I host a television show called, *Leadership Table Talk*. As the host, one of the most critical things that I do is <u>listen</u> to my guests and where the conversation is going. If I fail to listen, I will not learn about the topic or know how to adjust my questions if required.

As leaders, if you want to build an effective team, you must first practice listening, so that you can learn, and then engage in leading. This is what I refer to as the 3L Listening Model which is shown in Figure 5. It is difficult to lead if you don't know your team, or what the issues are. Great leaders know how to listen!

Some of the greatest comments I ever received from my staff were, "You are a great boss and a great listener. You care enough to listen to what **we** have to say, and then you give everyone an opportunity to speak."

One lady specifically said, "I noticed that you would always look around the room to see who was not speaking, then you would strategically engage them to ensure that their voice was heard." When she told me that she had adopted that same strategy as a military commander, I was humbled by her willingness to follow my lead. As a leader, you never know who you are inspiring.

The 3L Listening Model

Now, let's take a quick look at the 3L Listening Model. See Figure 5. Although there is a myriad of listening models, I wanted to expand on the <u>why</u> and

<u>how</u> we need to listen. This point was made abundantly clear to me in the military.

When I was first commissioned in the Air Force, I was a Second Lieutenant or what we refer to as a "brown or butter bar." This term of endearment meant that you were brand new to the service.

Figure 5: The 3L Listening Model

Imagine if I had arrived at my unit pretending to know everything there was to know about the Air Force, communications-electronics, maintenance, computers, operations, security, deployments, etc. I would have failed in that assignment. Although I was in charge in my specific area, I still had to *listen* to those non-commissioned officers who had knowledge that I did not possess. We were a team and had to function accordingly. Although I had graduated from the Basic Communications-Electronics Maintenance Officer's School at Keesler Air Force Base in Biloxi, Mississippi, I had to take my book knowledge and convert it into practical hands-on training. I had the theory, but now I needed to learn how to integrate it into my day-to-day activities. I had to *learn* so that I could later *lead* my team more effectively.

As a side-note, the famous Air Force astronaut, the late Lieutenant Colonel Michael P. Anderson was my classmate at Keesler. He had a degree in Physics, and I had a degree in Chemistry. Somehow, we both got assigned to the Air Force's Communications-Electronics Maintenance Officer career field. Although Michael was the *top graduate* in our class, he did not remain in the career field long. He later became an Air Force pilot and then a NASA astronaut. After seeing his name in the Air Force Times as part of the new astronaut class in 1994, I called his office at Rome Air Force Base in New York to congratulate him on his selection. Then in February of 2003, I saw the explosion of the Space Shuttle Columbia, it broke my heart. In addition to the others who tragically lost their lives, my classmate, and my friend was gone.

Please forgive the digression, but I thought you might enjoy that particular sidebar story. It is not often that one has the opportunity to attend school with an individual who would later fly aboard the NASA Space Shuttle.

Six Tips for Effective Listening

So, how can you become a more effective listener? Here are six tips. First, you need to listen with open ears and committed eyes. Have you ever tried talking to someone who had (a) already made up their mind, and (b) had wandering eyes? How did that make you feel? As a leader, remember that feeling the next time you engage in listening to one of your team members.

Second, refrain from being judgmental. If you are listening to learn, then you must resist the temptation of bringing your personal beliefs into the equation, until you have heard the other point of view. You are listening to learn not judge.

Third, clarify to understand. For example, you may say, "Charles, just to clarify, I believe this is what you said. Am I correct?

Fourth, don't allow body language to send negative signals. Crossed arms, dying to speak, are just two of the signals that can prevent listening. For example, if I am listening to you with my arms crossed, it could be a sign of anger. The signal that I am sending is that you are wasting my time, and I don't have time to listen.

Likewise, if you are engaged in a conversation and you *can't wait to speak*, it could be interpreted that you don't value the other person's views. If you want to build a team that is inclusive and values other's opinions, you have to learn to listen.

In a recent speech on *The Art of Listening*, I described the above behavior to the audience as "being disrespectful." One of the questions that I often ask, "Is your opinion so important, that you can't **wait** until the other person completes his or her thought?"

Effective listening is a two-way activity, not a one-way soapbox. When you are listening to learn, you need to refrain from trying to dominate the conversation or the environment. If you detect fear or apprehension in the other person, do your part to put them at ease. They could simply be nervous. As the leader, try to minimize their anxiety.

Fifth, don't commit to listen, if you don't have the time to "hear." Have you ever had to brief someone and they squirmed and talked throughout the entire presentation? Although you hoped that they were listening, you knew it was a futile effort.

Let me share a brief story. I was asked to give the command presentation to a high-ranking visitor. As a member of the command briefing team, it was a standard pitch that we gave routinely. Throughout the presentation, I observed that the visitor was talking, flipping papers, and not listening to a word that I said.

Yet, as I was completing the briefing, the visitor abruptly asked, *"Can you start over? I was talking and listening to my colleague."* I was shocked by his callous remarks and behavior.

At that time, my boss intervened and reminded the visitor of the agenda. Due to the tight aircraft schedule, we could not afford to give the briefing a second time, especially since we had a host of activities planned. I must admit that I did not want to brief this individual ever again. For this high-profile visitor, learning to listen was obviously not a requirement for leadership.

Finally, number six, remain objective, not critical. As leaders, you have to remain objective about any conversation that you may have with your team. Don't go into a conversation with blinders. You are the boss. You can listen with open ears. Even if you do not accept the perspective or proposal of the person speaking with you, don't criticize the other individual.

I witnessed this obtuse behavior first-hand several years ago. A government team had come to brief a group of senior leaders. Before the presenter got to his third slide, one of the senior leaders began to criticize the presentation profusely.

There was no way, this senior leader could have learned anything, because he was already convinced that this idea was flawed. As I sat through the presentation, I thought, "If this is how this senior leader treats individuals presenting information to him, then he is not a leader, but is simply occupying a space."

Getting to Know Your Organization

What is your organization's vision, mission, and core values? Are you and your team in sync with them? Several years ago, these entities were posted all over walls throughout organizations. As a result, there was no misunderstanding or confusion as to what they were. Even if people disagreed with them, at least they knew what they were.

However, as things changed, some employees began to complain that they were *strictly* for show, because numerous leaders failed to abide by them – especially the core values. In response, some organizations have minimized the importance of these three critical elements to the detriment of organization cohesiveness.

Yet, every successful leader knows that if you want to build a winning team, you must set the example that you want your team members to follow. Before a team ever buys into your organization, they must first believe in you and what you stand for.

Let me share a quick story. I was working with an organization several years ago. I spent some time asking employees about the vision. To my surprise, some of them did not know the leader's vision for the organization. He did not share it and they did not ask.

Then I asked about the mission of the organization.

The responses were just as complex. There was no clear understanding as to the purpose of the organization. This was a very interesting dynamic. History has shown that this kind of organization will not last, but eventually crumble due to a lack of cohesiveness.

Vision, Mission, and Core Values

In getting to know your organization, it is essential that you as the leader establish and clarify the _vision, mission,_ and _core values_ in the organization. As the leader, you set the tone and the direction for where the organization will go. There can be no ambiguity. You must be clear and concise, and intentional with your direction.

Your vision, mission, and core values should never become what I refer to on my television show as "wall art," but reflect the essence and cornerstone of your organization.

Here is one example of why this is important. With an extensive background in management coupled with certification in Lean Six Sigma, I was hired to guide an organization through the development of their strategic plan. I facilitated several "brainstorming" sessions that provided the foundation for conducting a strengths, weaknesses, opportunities, and threats (SWOT) analysis. The outputs of the analysis enabled the organization to refine its mission, vision, strategic goals, objectives, and short-term and long-term strategies.

Although the vision and mission statements were sound, there was one critical missing component. This strategic oversight could not be disregarded or ignored.

The organization had not developed or published a set of *core values* in which the team could acquiesce to.

You may wonder, "Why is this an issue? Core values represent the heartbeat of the organization, and the key convictions that energize performance. These values are integrated into the strategies that drive operations, policies, processes, and capital investment decisions. They are the linchpins that are weaved throughout the zip line of the organization. Core values gives employees a baseline moral code in which they can adopt as organizational guiding principles.

Yet, without a clear set of core values, leaders are missing a key ingredient to building an effective organization. In addition, the entire team has no organizational standards for measuring acceptable behaviors. If you ever wondered if core values matter. The answer is a resounding—yes.

What is Your Organizational Culture Story?

What does the success of Apple, Zappos, Southwest Airlines, Wal-Mart, Google, Facebook, and the Four Seasons Hotel have in common? The answer is "culture." Each of these companies have created an environment in which their organizational culture has generated a competitive advantage for the company.

Now, imagine if these companies' organizational culture was mired in behaviors that alienate, bully, and destroy teams. What kind of work climate would this be? Not only would the companies lose many of their valuable employees, they would also lose their customer base, revenues, and their industry standing.

A Leader's Role in Creating the Right Culture

As the leader in your organization, what kind of organizational culture are you creating? Do your core values promote people, trust, teamwork, quality, honesty, integrity, accountability, responsibility, innovation, quality, diversity, and inclusiveness?

Have you ever heard the old adage, "What you permit is what you allow and endorse?" According to Edgar Schein, an organizational development pioneer, and a Sloan Fellows Professor of Management Emeritus at the Sloan School of Management at the Massachusetts Technology Institute (MIT) "The only thing of real importance that leaders do is [to] create and manage culture." I purport that in order to effectively know your organization, leaders must understand the cultural dynamics in existence in the organization.

Organizational Culture Defined

So, what is organizational culture? Is it some obtuse idea? Based on the preponderance of organizational behavior literature, organizational culture is described as the "shared assumptions, values, and beliefs that guide the behaviors and actions of its members to include its leaders." According to Schein, there are three levels of culture:

1. Artifacts: Visible elements that represent the company (e.g. business processes),

2. Espoused values: Strategies, goals, and vision that define the organization, and
3. Assumptions and beliefs: Unconscious beliefs, perceptions, thoughts, and feelings manifested through personal behaviors.

Why Organizational Culture Matters?

In their groundbreaking work, *Diagnosing and Changing Organizational Culture Competing Values Framework*, Kim Cameron, and Robert Quinn used evidence-based research to describe how organizational culture can reveal behaviors, norms, and values operating within organizations.

The framework, which consists of four dominant culture types (Clan, Adhocracy, Market, and Hierarchy), provides leaders with statistical data for assessing the cultural dynamics operating in the organization. Each culture type represents explicit behaviors, artifacts, norms, and implicit assumptions.

So, why would this data be important in getting to know your organization? By understanding your organization's culture type to include subcultures, leaders can design the appropriate leadership strategy for implementing change. Without this detailed analysis, organizations can fall victim to *cultural misfit* – using a leadership strategy designed for a different organizational culture.

Additionally, if you fail to understand your organization's culture, you will make faulty assumptions, and implement flawed policies, procedures, and strategies that are contrary to the culture present in the organization.

To emphasize this point, let me share with you a few examples. When I was in the military, I led different types of organizations. Some units were comprised only of military, while others had a combination of military, government civilians, and contractors. Yet, in one organization, I was the only military.

In each of the above scenarios, I had to exercise a different leadership style in order to be effective. I could not get to know my organization using techniques that did not align with the organization's culture. When you are leading an all military unit, it is totally different than when you are leading a group of senior level government civilians or contractors. As leaders, we have to ensure that we understand the organizational culture in which we operate.

Organizational Culture and Cyber Security

You still may be wondering, "What is the big deal with organizational culture?" Let me answer that question by sharing with you an example that involves my background in information security and cyber security. As a former Chief Information Officer (CIO), this was a major part of my professional portfolio for many years.

In 2017, I completed a study at Georgetown University entitled, *Exploring Information Security Challenges Facing Federal Chief Information Security Officers (CISOs) Using the Competing Security Cultures Framework.* Yet, my interest in this topic spans decades.

While attending the Air Force Command and Staff College in 1996, I completed a capstone project entitled,

Information Warfare: Combating the Threat in the 21st Century. Based on my research, I opined that,

> Our nation's growing dependency on
> information and information-based
> technologies creates tremendous
> vulnerabilities in our national security
> infrastructure. A hostile adversary can
> wage information warfare attacks
> anonymously from the global sphere.
> These attacks can quickly paralyze a nation.

Yet, to fully understand how the cybersecurity example relates to understanding organizational culture, let me provide you with some context. First, let me ask you a few questions:

1. How many of you use some form of government services?
2. Is your personal identifiable information (PII) stored in the computers used by these government agencies, or is it in the cloud?
3. How secure are the networks, cloud infrastructures, etc.?
4. Have you ever been notified that there was a **<u>breach</u>** in one of these government networks?
5. Do you ever wonder about the employees who work at these agencies and whether they are exercising due diligence in protecting the information and the networks?
6. Do you think that having an organizational culture that fosters sound security practices is

critical to protecting your PII?

7. How would you feel if the culture at these agencies was free fall – anything goes?

If you answered yes to any of these questions, then I invite you to continue reading about the importance of establishing an effective information security and cyber security culture in organizations. Why? Because your personal data is at stake.

As background, although the Federal Information Security Modernization Act (FISMA) of 2014 compels federal agencies to implement an effective information security program, organizations are under siege by internal and external cyberattacks. In September 2016, the U.S. House of Representatives Committee on Oversight and Government Reform released a report indicating that the government "has never before been more vulnerable to cyberattacks. No agency appears safe."

Because cyber threats can cause critical harm to the United States national security, critical infrastructure, financial and health institutions, according to the government accountability office (GAO), federal chief information security officers (CISOs) face tremendous challenges in combating these threats. Yet, according to cyber experts, Paulsen and Coulson, "for an organization to be secure, there must be a _culture_ of information security."

In order for there to be a culture of information security, every employee must understand their role in ensuring that this culture is not violated. But, that is not always the case.

In a 2017 News 4 I-Team report, over 100 government

employees in 12 federal agencies <u>violated</u> their agency's security policies by using government computers to visit *pornographic websites*. On March 7, 2017, the US Central Intelligence Agency (CIA) had "8,761 [classified] documents" leaked to WikiLeaks. This leak followed Edward Snowden's 2013 disclosure of classified National Security Agency (NSA) documents also to WikiLeaks.

Although this specific example pertains to leaders in the information security and cyber security area, this information is not isolated to this group of professionals. By taking time to understand the security culture in the organization, federal agency CISOs can *identify competing values and behaviors* that may induce *risk* to the organization's information security goals and objectives.

As men and women who uses government provided services for various reasons, we should all want the culture in these agencies to be at peak performance.

Culture and Globalization

Now, let's extend culture beyond the four walls of your building and explore the global aspect of culture. For example, can your leadership behaviors alienate your team if you fail to understand different cultures? What do you think? I propose that the answer is yes.

With globalization on the increase, it is imperative that leaders understand the myriad of global and multicultural dynamics at work in organizations worldwide. The economic interdependency of global markets is pervasive. Karen Lawson, author of the book *Leadership Development Basics* writes, "As more and more companies do business internationally, the emphasis on developing leaders who can help their companies succeed in a global environment will increase."

As a leader, how you interact with your team (physical or virtual) will reveal much about your character and ability to lead. Bully leadership tactics will not work here. You have to value and respect the contributions of every team member regardless of their culture, nationality, background, or heritage.

Since many businesses are establishing a global footprint, developing leaders with high cultural intelligence is not a luxury, but a necessity. According to Dr. David Livemore, author of *The Cultural Intelligence Difference*, "The ability to understand different perspectives and adjust behaviors accordingly can be the deciding factor in whether teams work cohesively, deals are closed, and projects thrive." Investing time in learning about other cultures can prove the difference between business success and failure.

However, in order to effectively negotiate and collaborate with a global business in another country, you have to be cognizant of your own internal biases. They can cloud your judgment and block effective communications. You must remain aware of your behaviors, motives, and intent.

If you are going to lead without alienating, bullying, or destroying your team, you must also understand your proclivities to different things. Personal idiosyncrasies can create blind spots and prohibit leaders from learning how to effectively lead in a multicultural environment.

Lightbulb Moments

Jack Welch, Jr. once said, "Before you are a leader, success is all about growing yourself. When you become a leader, success is all about growing others." What a profound statement. It summarizes the essence of what I envisioned as *The Know Factor of Leadership*.

Throughout this chapter, I discussed the importance of getting to know you, your team, and your organization. You will never succeed at leading others if you cannot lead the person whose shadow is your own. Invest time in getting to know the "real" you.

As you get to know your team, develop your communications and listening skills. Choose the correct communications medium to deliver the right message at the right time, with the right motive and intent. But remember that your tone and emotional state has consequences when you are communicating with your team. As the leader, what you say and how you say it sets the tone for what is acceptable behavior in the organization.

Finally, getting to know your organization goes beyond vision, mission, and core values, because your *organizational culture* is a direct reflection of you.

7-Strategy #4

Commit to Full Throttle Leadership

When I was in college, I took my first airplane ride to Anaheim, California. I was one of several students selected from North Carolina Agricultural and Technical State University (NCA&TSU) in Greensboro, NC to attend the American Chemical Society Conference. As a chemistry major, this was a great opportunity for any student. However, as a teenager, getting the opportunity to go to Disney Land was even better.

Since I had never flown on an airplane, I was fascinated by how the pilot was able to regulate and control the power and altitude of the aircraft. A little confession, deep down, I have always been an engineer

79

at heart. Yet, prior to going to college, I never was exposed to women in engineering. If I had, I probably would have pursued an engineering degree.

 As I continued analyzing the airplane ride, I began to recall my studies in thermodynamics. By using the airplane's *throttle*, the pilot has an enormous amount of power at his or her fingertips.

Imagine setting at the controls—deciding how fast or slow you want the plane to go at that particular moment. As the pilot, you have an awesome amount of responsibility. Everybody onboard the aircraft is relying on you and your expertise to maneuver the plane correctly.

So, what happens at *full throttle*? At full throttle, the aircraft is expected to produce greater output or performance, and go further than it would at a lesser speed. As a teenager, I thought, "What an engineering design feat." The speed of this massive aircraft can be controlled to a certain degree by this device positioned between the pilot and the co-pilot.

Now, let's take a look at how this aircraft analogy can apply to leaders who desire to lead without alienating, bullying, or destroying their team. First, are leaders the pilots in their organizations? Second, can leaders control the performance of their team? Third, are leaders responsible for the culture in their organization? Finally, do leaders have the capacity to create a work environment that leverages the contributions of all team members? If you answered yes to any of these questions, then I invite you to continue reading.

What would happen if leaders committed to "Full Throttle Leadership?" Before I answer that question, let me define this form of leadership.

What is Full Throttle Leadership?

Full throttle leadership is proactive behaviors or measures that take an organization from ground zero to the right elevation, at the right speed, and for the right purpose. With precision, the leader moves the organizational needle from a place of independent action to team action.

Full throttle leaders are proactive. They don't wait until a situation approaches crisis mode before they act. These leaders have established mechanisms in place to guard against "surprises." By staying engaged with their team, listening, publishing pertinent policies, and providing avenues to address concerns, these leaders are choosing to engage full throttle.

Keen judgment, wise, and preceptive are terms also used to describe full throttle leaders. These leaders understand that in order to advance the organization, you have to be strategic in your thinking and planning. Just as military planners have to assess the entire battlefield prior to planning an operation, full throttle leaders must assess the behavioral blueprint of their organization. As a leader, ask yourself these questions, "What do I need to do to keep the organization on the right trajectory? Are changes necessary to produce the right results?" If changes must occur in the organization, they must be done right.

Full throttle leaders are not afraid to act. They are decision-makers who understand the consequences that result from no action. If there are behaviors either on the part of the leader or the staff that are threatening the existence of the organization, then this dynamic must change. No organization will survive under this canopy.

To better understand full throttle leadership, I developed a brief description for each alphabet. Organizations with full throttle leadership observe the following from their leader:

- F = Fearless; willing to take-charge and disrupt behaviors that are sabotaging the organization.
- U = Unity; willing to bond together to create a winning team versus independent silos.
- L = Loyalty; willing to defend what is right for the organization and more importantly, its #1 resource – its people.

- L = Likable; willing to work hard to create a work environment in which employees enjoy coming to work. There is nothing worse than coming to a job you dislike and a boss you distrust.
- T = Thankful; willing to thank and recognize others before he or she showers down rewards on themselves.
- H = Honesty; willing to engage in honest behaviors and promote them throughout the organization.
- R = Respect; willing to extend to others the same level of deference or admiration that he or she expects in return.
- O = Open-minded; willing to refrain from being closed-mined so that he or she can learn new ideas and gain different perspectives from a diverse workforce.
- T = Teachable; willing to maintain a teachable spirit. Leaders who are unwilling to learn from others will become blinded by their own unwavering mindset.
- T = Transformable; willing to transform from non-productive leadership behaviors to time-proven team-building behaviors that unify and strengthen organizations.
- L = Listener; willing to listen with "open ears." Leaders who practice the art of effective listening are more apt to make decisions based on informed data than personal bias.
- E = Encourager; willing to encourage, inspire, and motivate others to become their best both

on and off the job.

In addition to observing the above behaviors, full throttle leaders are magnets at attracting the kind of team members that will help to move the organization to the next level of positive performance. There is something about leaders who exude humility, confidence, and a genuine interest in helping and serving others. Because of their willingness and commitment to doing what is right in the organization, these leaders have a reputation based on solid principles and integrity.

Let me share a quick example. I worked for a boss who not only was a full throttle leader, but he conducted himself in such a way that people were clamoring to work for him. Since this boss was an *aviator*, I guess you could say that he was really a full throttle leader.

As a boss, this leader set the bar for other leaders to emulate. His reputation proceeded him. Everybody that I ever spoke to about this individual, had only good things to say. This in and of itself was amazing. How many people do you know have earned this kind of impeccable reputation?

I counted myself *blessed* to have had the opportunity to work for a person of his caliber. Because of his work ethic, he inspired me to want to give even more. He never asked his team to do anything that he was not willing to do himself. It was nothing for him to spend time talking with individuals at every level of the organizational chain. He did not discriminate based on your position in the organization. He treated everyone with the same level of respect that he afforded senior high-profile leaders.

Although I had several years of leadership and management experience under my belt at the time that I worked for this individual, I was still able to add to my leadership toolkit. I never want to arrive at the point in my leadership journey, that I will dismiss the teachings of other seasoned and experienced leaders. I am still using some of the leadership principles that I learned from that boss even today. As a proponent of leadership development training, I firmly believe in continuous growth, and education. If you want to grow as a leader, you have to be willing to learn.

So, as leaders, if you are promoting the right example through your actions and behaviors, you will be amazed at who is watching you and will want to join your team.

Lightbulb Moments

In this chapter, we explored the relationship between a pilot's aircraft throttle device and leadership. The goal of the discussion was to explain how leaders can control the level of performance that can occur in organizations when someone is in charge.

Below are some of the key take-aways:

- Full throttle leaders know how to steer the organization toward excellence. Settling at the door post of mediocrity is not a part of the equation.

- Full throttle leaders understand that it takes the right level of thrust to move the organization past ground zero. Over compensating for extenuating circumstances can introduce chaos and complexity when not evaluated correctly.
- Full throttle leaders are not afraid to act.
- Full throttle leaders are not self-centered.
- Full throttle leaders are not reactive but proactive. Through open lines of communications, these leaders keep their hands on the pulse of operations throughout their organization. By doing this, they can minimize surprises, and reduce grape-vine issues.
- Full throttle leaders are people builders, encouragers, and will push employees to maximum proficiency.
- Full throttle leaders are magnets for attracting the right talent to join their team. By setting the right leadership example, they are able to connect with team members at a level that disingenuous leaders cannot.
- Full throttle leaders are not afraid of change. However, these leaders know that change for change sake is not the answer. Making the right changes will produce the right results.

8 -Strategy #5
Own Your Leadership
Behavior

Several years ago, I spoke to the Washington, DC Web Women organization, which is a group of women technology professionals and thought-leaders. The theme of the presentation was *Owning Your Leadership Presence*. Having served in several senior technology leadership positions, I was asked to share my experiences and challenges with the group comprised primarily of millennials. Not only was this experience rewarding for me, but enlightening as well.

After laying the foundation for what leadership is and is not, I presented to the group some research documenting what others believe constitute a great leader. Based on an anonymous survey using random sampling and a mixture of open and closed-ended questions, I compiled a list of what respondents recognize as effective leadership characteristics. Although the results were typical of effective leaders (e.g. visionary, ethical, decision-maker, thought-leader, honest, values people, communicator, respectful, sets the right example), what I found most compelling is what respondents thought about ineffective leaders. See the list below:

- Lack of vision, integrity, honesty, and respect
- Unable to make decisions
- Unqualified for the position
- Unethical, lack morals and values
- Non-inspirational or motivational
- Unapproachable, non-trust worthy
- Self-absorbed, not a team player
- Close-minded, not open to new ideas
- Unable to delegate
- Fails to mentor or coach others
- Does not set a good example
- Poor communicator and listener

What Does it Mean to Own Your Leadership Behavior?

Although I could have spent an enormous amount of time speaking with the young ladies about effective leadership, I wanted to ensure that I addressed those areas that can disrupt and destroy organizations. The above list of negative attributes are the building blocks for confusion, discord, and chaos. Therefore, to avoid this calamity, leaders must own their leadership behavior. They must recognize when and where change in behavior is necessary to ensure organizational success.

As a leader, regardless of your experience or time in leadership, if your leadership style is characterized by the above behaviors, it will catapult you into the failure zone. Admitting that you may need help with your leadership development skills is not a sign of weakness. It represents a level of maturity which is expected of genuine leaders.

Unfortunately, many leaders have fallen victim to the negative leadership behaviors identified above. These leaders were unwilling to change or learn from others who had already walked this path. Experience is not always the best teacher, especially if you are willing to value and leverage the experience of others.

When it comes to owning your leadership behavior, I devised a short description that will help you remember this strategy. Let's look at OWN.

- O = Orchestrate your leadership behavior so that it aligns with and contributes to the good of the organization.
- W = Watch out for communications and situations that can generate toxic outcomes and destructive results.
- N = Never use your leadership position to engage in behaviors that violate the principles of honorable leadership.

Owning your leadership behavior is being

responsible for your role in creating an organization that values and respects others. It is leading from a place of intentionality. If you want to create a work environment that may one day make the Best Places to Work list, then you have to be intentional with how you lead. For example, are you holding employees accountable for bad behaviors that are threatening the work climate at your organization? Are you following up on complaints in a timely manner, or are you ignoring them believing that they will go away?

As a leader, owning your leadership behavior is resolving conflicts before they become mountains. It is conducting conversations with individuals that may disagree with your position, but deserve to be heard. It is being the first person to take responsibility for what occurs under your watch. Passing the buck is not an option for leaders who desire to lead from the front.

Owning your leadership behavior demands that you as the leader take-charge of the actions that occur in your organization. It is not delegating your responsibility to a lower level office, but it is standing firm in your position as leader. Although many people desire to lead, few understand the level of demand it places on your shoulders. Leadership is not for the faint of heart.

> "It is not what you do when the sun is shining, and people are showering down praise, but it is what you do as a leader, when everything has hit the fan, and you are trying to bring calm out of chaos."

As the leader, what you do does matter. If you believe otherwise, you have been misinformed. Your decisions will be scrutinized up and down the chain. Likewise, your leadership behavior will either result in an organization that is climbing and ascending, or collapsing and descending.

Let me share one quick story. As a military commander, you go on a number of training missions or exercises. In preparation for the deployment, you plan everything down to the nth degree. One writer once said that "Every plan is good until it encounters the enemy." Although we were going on an exercise, I thought that I had every detail covered. I trusted one of my staff members to pack a particular work item that I would need for the deployment. When I asked the member for it, he regrettably told me that he had forgot to pack it. Although I would have preferred to have had the equipment, the deployment was not the place or the time to share my disappointment. I had to revector my focus, proceed with what I had, and move out accordingly.

Imagine what would have happened if I had proceeded to go off on the military member? With the tension of the deployment already in the air, the morale would have suffered tremendously. My team and I had enough to keep us busy without having to deal with an out-of-control leader!

Lightbulb Moments

What are some of the take-aways that leaders can gleam from this chapter?

- Leaders are responsible for owning their behavior. They are entrusted with a certain level of trust and are expected to honor that code of ethics.
- There are some leadership behaviors that are ineffective, and are more prone to creating toxic work environments.
- Although leaders can hold employees accountable for specific work functions, leaders cannot delegate their leadership responsibilities.
- Leaders who own their leadership behavior are willing to act to address those issues that can create internal splits and wedges in the organization.

Conclusion

Your Change Begins Now

In their New York Times bestseller book, *Influencer: The Power to Change Anything*, Patterson, Grenny, Maxfield, McMillan, and Switzler reminds us that when it comes to change, "...there is no one strategy — no silver bullet for resolving profound, persistent, and resistant problems." As I read this, I thought about how leaders who desire to build effective teams, must be willing to explore many strategies that will prevent a toxic work environment.

With workplace bullying at an all-time high, learning how to lead without alienating, bullying, or destroying your team is a skill that every leader and manager must learn. Gone are the days of *code of silence*. Employees are responding to this dilemma with their feet. Employee turn-over rates are soaring leaving organizations scrambling to recruit, train, and retain the right talent.

Yet, if the organizational culture is toxic, then this task may prove unsurmountable. As indicated earlier, according to the Workplace Bullying Institute, 61% of bullies are bosses, which puts the time for change at critical mass! There are no options. If organizations are going to succeed, there can be no place for Dr. Jekyll and Mr. Hyde leadership operatives.

Rogue leaders who abuse their power, authority, and position will eventually destroy the team and the organization. Without a leadership intervention, they will continue to conduct business as usual collecting casualties along the way. These misguided leaders are engaging in leadership deception. They have fallen victim to what I call *Leadership FOG*.

Throughout this book, I identified five different strategies that leaders can use to include various models. In addition to resisting the temptations associated with Leadership FOG, I discussed the need to avoid creating discord, dysfunction and disillusionment in organizations. The third strategy, which was probably the most in-depth, emphasized the importance of getting to know you, your team, and your organization.

In getting to know the organization, leaders cannot dismiss the role of culture. Leaders are responsible for establishing the right culture in the organization. What you permit is in essence, what you are allowing to take place—under your watch.

The fourth strategy that I proposed encouraged leaders to commit to full throttle leadership. Just as pilots engage the throttle to adjust the power and altitude of the aircraft, full throttle leaders can adjust how they interact with their organizations to inspire peak performance. When leaders inject the right amount of influence and guidance, they can create a better outcome and result.

The final strategy that I recommended invited leaders to own their leadership behavior. Because there are some behaviors that are more prone to creating hostile work environments, leaders cannot take these behaviors for granted. Leaders are responsible for the actions that they take throughout the organization. These actions will be scrutinized up and down the chain. Although leaders can delegate accountability to employees, they can never delegate their responsibility as the leader in the organization. Therefore, leaders must behave in a manner that promotes good order and discipline in the organization.

Throughout the book, I reminded leaders to never take for granted that on the other side of every action that you initiate is a human being. Your leadership style, and communications do matter. What you say and do has consequences.

As leaders, I challenge you to commit to using your leadership position to influence for the greater good. Don't abuse your power or authority. Don't allow your ego to circumvent your judgment. Instead, decide to change your mindset so that you can elevate your leadership abilities.

To help you with your decision to lead without alienating, bullying, or destroying your team, I compiled a final list of questions that I hope you will consider and take time to answer. They are designed to help you evaluate your leadership behaviors.

Questions to Consider:

1. As the leader in your organization, are you engaging in workplace bullying tactics?

2. As the leader in your organization, are you permitting workplace bullying behaviors to take place between co-workers?

3. As the leader in your organization, what kind of organizational culture are you endorsing?

4. As the leader in your organization, are you setting the right example for your team?

5. As the leader in your organization, are your motives and intentions correct?

6. As the leader in your organization, are you engaging in leadership FOG?

7. As the leader in your organization, are you contributing to discord, dysfunction, and disillusionment among your employees?

8. As the leader in your organization, are you misusing the power that has been afforded you based on your position?

9. As the leader in your organization, are you showing acts of favoritism to certain individuals?

10. As the leader in your organization, are you mentoring specific individuals while neglecting others?

11. As the leader in your organization, are you using different sets of standards to administer discipline and punishment for the same offenses to different groups?

12. As the leader in your organization, is your word

your bond?

13. As the leader in your organization, are you able to separate leadership from friendship?

14. As the leader in your organization, are you threaten by the performance of any of your subordinates?

15. After reading this book, are there specific leadership behaviors that you need to change to be a more effective leader?

Although the above questions appear direct, they are designed to assist you in identifying potential behaviors that may be blocking you from being the best leader that you can be. Since leaders have an obligation to create a healthy and safe work environment for their team, there can be no compromise when it comes to doing the right thing. Leaders must be proactive. Zig Ziglar once said, "People don't care how much you know, until they see how much you care."

For leaders who want to build successful organizations without destroying their team in the process, they must adhere to effective leadership principles. For example, people are the nucleus to any organization. Successful and effective leaders recognize their limitations and are not afraid to develop others. These leaders are not threatened by the outstanding performance of their subordinates. They recognize the leadership potential and are willing to allow it to grow. When leaders take care of their people, they will respond in kind. Implementing a healthy, vibrant, and progressive work culture can generate enormous returns for the organization. For example, some companies have created competitive advantage in their organizations based on how they treat their employees. When employees feel valued, respected, and appreciated, they will identify better with the organization than if the opposite was true.

As discussed in the book, employees who believe that the work culture is toxic and that the leader has no interest in his or her growth or development, will leave. There is a host of research to substantiate this assertion. Employees, especially those with marketable skills are not staying in organizations where they are not appreciated and are undervalued.

Now suppose this script was flipped. Imagine if there were organizations in which leaders valued and respected their employees and vice versa. This would be a different world. Respect would be the "catch phrase" of the day. There is nothing wrong with being an optimist. It beats the alternative.

When I was at Georgetown, one of my favorite classes involved scenario planning. This planning primarily consists of developing "what-if" scenarios that may impact long and short-term business operations. Using a myriad of decision-making factors (e.g. political, financial, technological, international), different scenarios were generated. This futuristic planning enables business leaders to make informed business decisions.

As I recall this training, I began to imagine, "What would happen if leaders began examining their leadership behavior against positive and negative long-term outcomes on the organization? What would happen if leaders began to put the people before themselves?" Imagine a scenario in which *What's In It For Me* (WIIFM) no longer applied to either the leader or the employee. But then, that is wishful thinking.

I often wonder about the example that we as experienced, seasoned leaders are setting for the next generation. Is winning that business deal at any cost – everything? Why do we need to leave our values (e.g. integrity, respect, honesty, morality) at the door of our office complex? Since some leaders have no problem doing this, then why would we expect the next generation of leaders to do any different. They are watching us!

So, in closing, I wrote this book to challenge the leadership behaviors that are crippling organizations today. By integrating real-world case studies coupled with research and practical advice, I wanted to deliver easy-to-implement strategies and models that will strengthen teams, build effective organizations, and help any leader avoid the toxic behaviors that alienate, bully, and destroy teams.

My final thought is this: *"When leaders learn to lead from a mindset of compassion and respect for others, they are primed to become the "influencers" who will one day change the course of history."*

Appendix A:

Key Findings: Workplace Bullying Institute 2017 Study

- 19% of Americans are bullied, another 19% witness it
- 61% of Americans are aware of abusive conduct in the workplace
- 60.4 million Americans are affected by it
- 70% of perpetrators are men; 60% of targets are women
- Hispanics are the most frequently bullied race
- 61% of bullies are bosses, the majority (63%) operate alone
- 40% of bullied targets are believed to suffer adverse health effects
- 29% of targets remain silent about their experiences
- 71% of employer reactions are harmful to targets
- 60% of coworker reactions are harmful to targets
- To stop it, 65% of targets lose their original jobs
- 77% of Americans support enacting a new law

Appendix B:
Strategies Summary One Sheet

Strategy 1: Resist Leadership FOG

- False Humility
- Obsessed with Power
- Guided by Ego

Strategy 2: Avoid the 3D Leadership Syndrome

- Discord
- Dysfunction
- Disillusionment

Strategy 3: Conquer the Know Factor of Leadership

- Getting to Know You
- Getting to Know Your Team
- Getting to Know Your Organization

Strategy 4: Commit to Full Throttle Leadership

Strategy 5: Own Your Leadership Behavior

Appendix C:
Case Studies Summary

Chapter 2: Where Does Bullying Start?

- The Subtle Bully – Kia's Story

Chapter 3: Leaders Gone Awry

- The Mad Director
- Bully Uncover – Gary's Story
- The Invisible Man

Chapter 4: Resist Leadership FOG

- False Humility – Hypothetical Example
- When Ego Subverts Action – Carla's Story

Chapter 5: Avoid the 3D Leadership Syndrome

- The Heartless Bully – Karen's Story

Chapter 6: Conquer the Know Factor of Leadership

- The Power of a Note – Whitney's Story

Appendix D:

10 Tips for Leading on Purpose

- Be Intentional

- Be Clear

- Be Focused

- Be Honest

- Be Positive

- Be Direct

- Be Aware

- Be Decisive

- Be Proactive

- Be Smart

References

Arbinger Institute. (2010). *Leadership and Self-Deception: Getting Out of the Box*. San Francisco: Berrett-Koehler Publishers, Inc.

Cameron, K.S., & Quinn, R.E. (2011). *Diagnosing and Changing Organizational Culture: Based on the Competing Values Framework*, 3rd Ed. San Francisco: Jossey-Bass.

Deloitte. (2016). *Global Human Capitol Trends Report*. https://www2.deloitte.com/insights/us/en/foc us/human-capital-trends/2016/human-capital-trends-introduction.html

Foster, D. (2012). *After Mandela: The Struggle for Freedom in Post-Apartheid South Africa*. New York. Liveright Publishing Corporation.

Gibbs, J. (2002). *Racing to Win: Establish Your Game Plan for Success*. Sisters, Oregon: Multnomah Publishers, Inc.

Goldsmith, M. (2007). *What Got You Here Won't Get You There*. New York. Hyperion.

Goleman, D. (2006). *Emotional Intelligence: Why It Can Matter More Than IQ*. New York: Bantam Dell.

Lawson, K. (2008). *Leadership Development Basics*. Alexandria, VA. ASTD Training Basics Series ASTD Press.

London, M. (1999). *Principled Leadership and Business Diplomacy: Values-Based Strategies for Management Development*. Quorum Books, Westport, Connecticut.

Mandela, N. (2010). *Long Walk to Freedom: The Autobiography of Nelson Mandela*. New York. Back Bay Books, Little Brown and Company.

Maxwell, J. (2011). *The 5 Levels of Leadership*. New York: Center Street.

McDermott, M. (2016). *Lecture Briefings* at Georgetown, University. Washington, DC.

Miller, J.G. (2010). *Outstanding! 47 Ways to Make Your Organization Exceptional*. New York: G.P. Putnam's Sons Publishers.

Morrison, E.K. (1994). *Leadership Skills: Developing*

Volunteers for Organizational Success. Fisher Books.

Mortensen, K.W. (2013). *Maximum Influence* (2nd Edition). New York: AMACOM.

Patterson, K., Grenny, J., Maxfield, D., McMillan, R., & Switzler, A. (2008). *Influencer: The Power to Change Anything.* New York: McGraw Hill.

Paulsen, C., & Coulson, T. (2011). *Beyond awareness: Using business intelligence to create a culture of information security.* Communications of the International Information Management Association (IIMA), Volume 11, Issue 3.

Schein, E.H. (2010). *Organizational Culture and Leadership,* 4th Ed. San Francisco: Jossey-Bass.

Stevenson, R.L. *The Strange Case of Dr. Jekyll and Mr. Hyde.*

Workplace Bullying Institute (June, 2017). 2017 WBI U.S. Workplace Bullying Survey June 2017. http://www.workplacebullying.org/wbiresearch /wbi-2017-survey/

About the Author

A graduate of the McDonough School of Business at Georgetown University, Dr. Mary M. Gillam is the owner of Executive Leadership Enterprise & Management Services, LLC which is a woman, and veteran-owned small business. With over 30+ years of leadership, management, and information technology experience, Dr. Gillam is a retired Air Force Colonel and former member of the Senior Executive Service (SES) Corps with the Department of Defense at the Pentagon. She is also a former business consultant with Booz Allen Hamilton, a major international consulting firm. In addition, Dr. Gillam was elected to serve on the Fairfax Public Access (FPA) Board. She is the Board Secretary and the Director of Strategic Planning.

The recipient of several civic and military awards, Dr. Gillam has led numerous award-winning organizations. As the host of the local television show, "Leadership Table Talk", Dr. Gillam has a passion for helping people maximize their team performance, increase their organization productivity, and align their strategic goals with their revenue projections.

Having lived in Europe, Dr. Gillam has served as the keynote speaker in several venues. She is a certified John Maxwell Team leadership, speaker, coach, and trainer. Certified in Lean Six Sigma, Dr. Gillam is also a Green Belt in management and organizational development.

As a former Chief Information Officer (CIO) and

Director of Technology, Innovation, and Engineering, Dr. Gillam is a strong proponent of science, technology, engineering, and math (STEM). Using her technical prowess, Dr. Gillam invented the new corporate leadership training tool, "The Leadership Build Zone." In addition to being named 1/6 finalists in a nation-wide Innovation Cup competition, Dr. Gillam was recently interviewed by Jack Canfield, co-author of the Chicken Soup of the Soul series, describing the unique attributes of this innovative game.

An Amazon #1 best-selling author of 12 books, Dr. Gillam is the author of other leadership books to include *"Gifted to Lead: 4 Steps to Releasing Your Leadership Potential."* She is also the creator of the C.O.R.E Leadership Development Model.

The Real Back Story

Imagined being married at 14 and giving birth to 17 children, and widowed at age 48. If that is not enough, you are now given sole responsibility for four of your little grandchildren, all under the age of six. Not only was that the story of Dr. Mary Gillam's paternal grandmother, Dr. Gillam was one of those little grandchildren.

Although, she did not have much, Dr. Gillam's grandmother was a Christian who trusted in God to provide for her and her family. Despite going blind later in life, she would often say, "I have never seen the righteous forsaken or its seed begging bread."

With only a fourth-grade education, Dr. Gillam's grandmother encouraged her children and grandchildren to pursue their education. Believing that God would make a way for her to pursue her goals, Dr. Gillam took her grandmother's advice and began a journey of growth and learning that continues today.

A Christian herself, Dr. Gillam believes that when you put God first, nothing is impossible.

About ELEMS

Executive Leadership Enterprise and Management Services (ELEMS) provides consultation services to government, corporate, non-profits, and professionals. ELEMS specializes in the areas of leadership, management, organizational development, strategic planning, and information technology assessment. The company offers a wide range of professional services all designed to help our clients maximize their team performance, increase organizational productivity, and align their strategic goals with revenue projections. Our services include:

- Consulting
- Coaching (1-on-1, Group)
- Training Seminars
- Workshops

- Speaking Services (Keynote, Break-out Sessions, Conferences)
- Lunch and Learn
- Webinars
- Masterminds

Our Mission

To deliver the highest quality management consulting services that enable our clients to grow and develop their human capital, maximize their organizational effectiveness, and improve their productivity.

Our Customers

The target audience for Executive Leadership Enterprise and Management Services is business owners, local, state, and federal government, human capital directors, program and project managers, corporate and government training/learning centers, business schools, non-profits, and professionals.

What Drives ELEMS

ELEMS tagline is *"Developing Solutions, Sharing Knowledge, Delivering Results."* The business is based on three vital components:

1. ELEMS thrives on developing a "win-win" relationship with its clients, partners, and team.
2. ELEMS seeks to create a tangible return on

investment (ROI) for the clients, leaving them better off for having engaged the company's services.

3. ELEMS strives to be a "value-add" to its clients, and not just a one and done company. We want our services to help our clients reach their goals.

For more information, please check out our website at https://www.executiveleadershipbiz.com.

Unique Training Products

A product that has captured the attention of many leadership

experts is *The Leadership Build Zone*®. Selected one of six products (out of 68 entrants nationwide) in the 2017 Veteran Women Inspiring the Spirit of Entrepreneurship Innovation Cup Competition, *The Leadership Build Zone*® educational board game is the first of its kind. This fun, innovative, and educational learning and development tool is designed to introduce in a fun environment, basic leadership development concepts and team-building principles to emerging leaders.

During a 2017 mastermind session in Santa Barbara, CA., with Jack Canfield, co-author of the international bestsellers, *Chicken Soup of the Soul* series, Dr. Gillam was interviewed about this dynamic new leadership training tool.

Figure 6: Jack Canfield & Mary Gillam

In addition to the game, Dr. Gillam has developed a Facilitator's Guide to accompany this product. Recognizing the need for continuous leadership development especially with emerging leaders, this product is great for team building exercises, one-on-one leadership training, conferences, etc.

The author of several books, one of Dr. Gillam's most popular requests is her book, Gifted *to Lead: 4 Steps to Releasing Your Leadership Potential* which is available on Amazon or the author's website: https://www.executiveleadershipbiz.com.

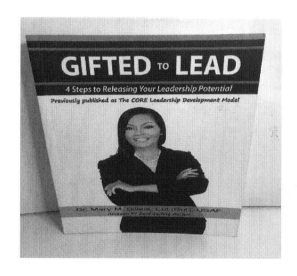